# MORRISTOWN

## A MILITARY HEADQUARTERS
## OF THE AMERICAN REVOLUTION

*This is how the Gilded Age ended. These crowds gathered at the auction at Florham, the mansion of Ruth Vanderbilt Twombly, great-granddaughter of Commodore Cornelius Vanderbilt. More than 13,000 persons attended the two-day auction, which netted $340,000.*

THE
# MAKING OF AMERICA
SERIES

# MORRISTOWN

## A MILITARY HEADQUARTERS
## OF THE AMERICAN REVOLUTION

## JOHN W. RAE

ARCADIA
PUBLISHING

Copyright © 2002 by John W. Rae
ISBN 978-0-7385-2400-9

Published by Arcadia Publishing,
Charleston SC, Chicago IL, Portsmouth NH, San Francisco CA

Printed in the United States

Library of Congress control number: 2002108725

For all general information contact Arcadia Publishing at:
Telephone 843-853-2070
Fax 843-853-0044
E-Mail sales@arcadiapublishing.com
For customer service and orders:
Toll-Free 1-888-313-2665

Visit us on the Internet at www.arcadiapublishing.com

FRONT COVER: *Whippany Farms is the estate of George G. Frelinghuysen, president of P. Ballantine and Sons Brewery, on Whippany Road. It is now the headquarters of the Morris County Park Commission.*

# CONTENTS

# ACKNOWLEDGMENTS

This is the record of the cultural, financial, and social heritage, unique and dramatic, of Morristown, New Jersey: its early settlers, the Revolutionary War encampments, the industrial revolution, the incorporation of the town in 1865, the erection of great mansions, the construction of towering office buildings where estates once stood, and the formation of its government. It is not the work of one person, but of a long list of individuals, historical societies, libraries, and town and National Historical Park archivists who expressed enthusiastic support for telling the tale in story and illustration.

It is not just confined to the area that comprises the town today. Rather, it engulfs the greater Morristown area once known as West or New Hanover and Morris Township, an area where industrial plants, office buildings, and suburban housing and apartment developments today vie for space.

It is a tale compiled from yellowed newspaper clippings, family archives, official records, and conversations with historians and officials who today are molding the new Morristown.

Too many illustrations and factual data were destroyed or lost that record Morristown's historic past and its rise to a modern shopping, banking, legal, and financial center. Fire destroyed one large collection of images in the 1930s. Others of the mansions, parties, fires, buildings, early industries, and work that made Morristown what it is today were never taken to tell the story of a lost era. It is sad, but the steady march of suburbanization and demand for land for office buildings, apartment complexes, and subdivisions came first.

Many have helped me with the often complex problems of gathering and verifying the materials of this economic and social history that relate the tale in detail of the change from farmland and woods to suburbia. I would like to especially thank the staff of the Joint Free Public Library of Morristown and Morris Township, the *Daily Record*, the Town of Morristown engineering department, the archivist at Delbarton School, the Morristown National Historical Park, who assisted in gathering both photographs and data, and John W. Rae Jr., who proofread the manuscript.

John W. Rae

# INTRODUCTION

Morristown throbs with the pulse of destiny, past and present, from that date nearly 300 years ago when the footprints of the Lenni Lenape Native Americans were the only sign of man traversing the wooded hillsides sloping to the Whippany River, to its place today as the banking, legal, commercial, and shopping hub of northern New Jersey.

Herein are contained the drama and pathos of a great sweep of events, illuminating sidelights, oddities, and amusing trifles of history, all of which combine to present a full image of the greater Morristown area, first known as West or New Hanover, then Morris Township.

Because of its historic past, Morristown was named by the National Trust for Historic Preservation as one of America's Top 12 Distinctive Destinations in July 2002. In making the nomination, the Trust cited Morristown's historic treasures, including Morristown National Historical Park, Historic Speedwell Village, and the home of Thomas Nast, one of the great caricaturists of the Golden Age of Illustration.

It was here that General George Washington encamped the Continental Army during two critical winters of the Revolutionary War, 1777–1778 and 1779–1780, actions that gave the then-tiny hamlet the title of "A Military Headquarters of the American Revolution" and led to the establishment of the nation's first National Historic Park here in 1933.

Here Benedict Arnold was tried for treason in the Dickerson Tavern; Lafayette returned from France in 1780 to report a powerful French fleet en route with help; Washington ordered the nation's first mass inoculation for smallpox to combat the disease rampant among the troops; Alexander Hamilton courted Betsy Schuyler; and two experienced soldiers, Baron Von Steuben and General Nathanial Green, whipped the inexperienced troops suffering from nakedness, cold, hunger, and bleakness into a formidable fighting force.

Growth was slow after the Revolutionary War. The tiny farming village of 250 persons General Washington brought his troops to in 1777 developed slowly into a rural shopping center, its shops hardly able to supply the wants of its population.

Its center was The Green, at first a grazing ground for cattle and sheep, around which many of the main buildings of the business district cluster. At first, it was churches, the first dating to 1718, then hotels and shops, banks, department stores, a newspaper office, and the post office. It was the site of the first Morris County Courthouse, the Liberty Pole, gaol, gallows, school, and a rustic bandstand. In 1871, a Civil War monument was added. It is now a park.

It was here that the early development of the telegraph occurred when Samuel F.B. Morse and Alfred Vail, his student at New York University, strung 3 miles of copper-covered milliner's wire around the barn in which they were working and in 1838 transmitted the first message: "A patient waiter is no loser."

From Morse's invention of the telegraph to basic research for Telstar communications satellites, Morristown has proved a fertile ground for inventive genius and research and development facilities. In 1823, George Macculloch, a Morristown millionaire, while fishing at Lake Hopatcong visualized and promoted a canal across New Jersey from Phillipsburg on the Delaware River to Jersey City on the Hudson River. Here great strides were made in preventive medicine by pharmaceutical laboratories and half-tone cuts were first successfully produced electronically by George Washington Jr., only son of the inventor of instant coffee and broth.

The Civil War over, Morristown bounded forward in strides that traversed every field of endeavor. In 1865, it petitioned the state legislature for a charter of incorporation as a town. The railroad was extended to Morristown, public and private schools were built, the gas works that produced gas to illuminate homes gave way to the Jersey Central Power and Light Company, the breakup of the large estates became subdivisions of homes, and TV's first variety show originated from Bell Telephone Laboratory's experimental radio station.

By the turn of the century, the village became the core of the richest and least-known colony of wealthy people in the world. It was a period of massive movements and of social and architectural splendor beyond the realm of Aladdin's wildest dreams that almost overnight changed Morristown into an "inland Newport."

There was no limit to the means these men and women of wealth would pursue to satisfy their claim to high society. Initially, many families with names like Vanderbilt, Kountze, Wolff, Higgins, Claflin, Dodge, James, Allen, and Twombly moved to Morristown to escape the summer heat of New York, living at first in leased residences. Then slowly a pattern emerged of construction and formation that witnessed the erection of vast estates and the creation of a country society.

By the 1930s, the wealthy were faced with soaring tax bills, the result of the introduction of the income and inheritance taxes; the Depression; skyrocketing maintenance costs; and a dwindling reservoir of good, inexpensive help and so they began to raze their mansions one after another. By the mid-1930s, almost half of the great homes were gone.

Industry, experimental laboratories, and world headquarters were the magnets that drew the influx of population to Morristown, whose business center has changed drastically since World War II. Gone is the town's first skyscraper, the five-story Babbitt Building, replaced by the five towers of Headquarters Plaza that eradicated stores on one side of Speedwell Avenue. The open-air parking lots on Cattano Avenue have been replaced by a parking garage and a huge apartment complex. Other apartment complexes and townhouses are under construction or proposed.

In the two decades following World War II, veterans were spurred by the GI Bill, which provided low cost mortgages, and middle income people from the central cities took advantage of the direct rail link to Morristown and gave the town the title "bedroom community." The breakup of the big estates into subdivisions and the construction of apartment and condominium complexes provided the housing.

It wasn't long before light industry and commercial establishments, aware of the skilled labor pool in the area, were attracted. Slowly, highly sophisticated industries and research-oriented facilities were hiring residents who formerly took the train to the inner city. The population of the town and township soared as subdivision after subdivision was approved. During the 1960s, 16 estates were divided into housing developments in the township and several garden apartment complexes were erected. By 1980, the trend toward condominiums and townhouses was well under way.

Land-starved Morristown, which sits in the hole of a doughnut surrounded by the township, was running out of land for large scale development. By the 1980s, the township population exceeded that of the town, whose population had stabilized at 18,544.

By the turn of the twenty-first century, the appearance of the business district began to change. Large scale apartment development appeared on Washington Street and Catano Avenue and a townhouse development appeared in the town's historic district. Morristown is continuing to change with the times.

*Charles J. Ogden painted early Morristown in 1820 from Fort Nonsense hill, showing the steeple of the First Presbyterian Church, The Green, and the few buildings of the time.*

# 1. THE FIRST SETTLERS

More than 300 years ago, the footprints of the Lenni Lenape Native Americans, the forebears of an expanding population that today has changed the greater Morristown area from rural to suburban, were the only sign of man traversing the Minnisink Trail or living by the Whippany River. The first to follow them were trappers from New Amsterdam, then came the early settlers from Newark, Elizabeth, Long Island, and New England, attracted by the good, rich farmland, excellent water supply, and rich iron ore deposits.

Like all cities, Morristown was not built in a day. In the early 1700s, the pioneers worked early and late clearing the forests of oak, elm, and pine trees, uprooting tree stumps, and moving rocks to clear the land to cultivate crops, plowing the rich soil, planting seed, harvesting the fruits of their endeavors, and building first log huts then frame homes.

It is uncertain when the first house was built by these early settlers, many of them drawn to the area by the lure of iron ore found in the hills. It stood, no doubt, near the banks of the Whippany River where a grist mill, sawmill, and forge were soon erected. The Native Americans had not then disappeared from the region, wild game abounded, and bears, wolves, and panthers roamed the forests.

The Lenni Lenape were a friendly and peaceful tribe who hunted the deer, but disliked farming. They selected dry, protected areas near water in which to camp. One such site, tradition says, was at the intersection of Park Avenue and Columbia Road.

The Native Americans did not remain long after the white man entered the region. The farm settlements hindered their hunting and fishing grounds. Many of their paths became roads, first dirt, then macadam. Typical are Whippany Road, Park Avenue, parts of Morris Street, and Morris Avenue.

By 1738, the village, if it might be called such, was centered mainly in Water Street though Morris Street might have boasted of an occasional hut, and two or three might have been found on what is now The Green. Sheep and cattle were brought into pens for the night for protection from the wild animals. Roads were scarcely known. An overgrown path, beside which was a mill, blacksmith shop, and two dwellings in three separate clearings, was all that led through Washington Valley to Mendham. There was scarcely a better route to Basking Ridge.

*This image is of the residence of General John Doughty on Mt. Kemble Avenue prior to the Revolutionary War. His estate overlooked a vast farm.*

In Morristown, first known as West or New Hanover, 5,711 acres were acquired by proprietors John Kay, Thomas Stevenson, John Helby, Hannah Scott, and Thomas Lambert as a result of the Indian purchase of 1713, the area of which stretched eastward from the Delaware River to Morris County. Kay's tract, 2,000 acres in size, included what is now The Green and Washington's headquarters.

For this vast piece of land the Native Americans received 4 guns, 40 silver shillings, 5 kettles, 4 shirts, 4 blankets, 5 coats, 10 quarts of powder, 40 lead bars, 2 knives, 10 hoes, 10 hatchets, 100 flints, and 6 gallons of rum.

In 1727, there were only three families living in Morristown, their crude houses clustered in the hollow along the Whippany River near Spring and Water Streets. After 1730, Morristown gained settlers in increasing numbers. Typical was Jacob Ford who in 1731 acquired 220 acres from the Kay tract and later built a house on it.

In the pre-Revolutionary War years, Morristown, though sparsely populated, became the center of a growing farming and agriculture community as more and more land was cleared, fenced, and plowed for new crops. These crops in turn necessitated the construction of mills using the water power of nearby streams to grind the corn and grain, most of which was used by the farmers to feed cattle or barter in town.

To the north of Morristown were the estates of the Hathaway and Johnes families; to the east, those of the Fords, who built the mansion General George

Washington used as his headquarters in 1779 and 1780; to the south, those of General John Doughty; and to the west, those of Silas Condict and his brothers.

Stores, though offering only a small line of goods, developed from the earliest days. The storekeepers usually had a farm or a trade to augment the meager income from the store. Sales were by barter since people had little or no money. Farmers drove into town with their butter, eggs, honey, or anything salable, taking in return articles which they could not produce on their farm.

By the time of the revolution, Morristown had several well stocked stores facing The Green or in The Hollow. The goods carried offered an interesting comparison to those of today. Typical were those advertised by Stephenson & Canfield:

> coarse broad cloths, coatings, scarlet cloth for cloaks, Irish linen, muslins, cambrick, shoes, stockings, beaver, castor and wood hats, sewing silk of all colors, fine thread, pins, needles, playing cards, penknives, pipes, knives and forks, ink powder, gun powder, snuff, tobacco, buttons, indigo, ivory and horn combs, coffee, scissors, silver shoe and knee buckles, thimbles, brass kettles and salt.

Other items for sale at various stores included wallpaper, window glass, soap, chalk, spectacles, writing paper, ink stands, almanacs, spelling books, clocks, corks, guns, powder, and shot.

*The road to Basking Ridge (Route 202) was hardly more than a dirt path, winding its way between fenced farm fields following old Native American trails, prior to the Revolutionary War.*

Manufacturing increased steadily in Morristown. During the Revolution, the town had several silversmiths, saddlers, watch repairmen, and a chaise maker. Help-wanted advertisements sought cutlers, gunsmiths, locksmiths, brass founders, and file cutters.

Before a house could be built, these first settlers had to make a clearing in the forest by cutting down the trees and leaving the stumps to decompose, or remove them. These clearings were usually located at one corner of the farm, rather than in the center. A cellar was dug in order to provide a warmer house and a place for frost-free storage. The cellar floor was dirt, but the walls were of stone gathered in the fields and laid together with mud or clay. The house itself was first constructed of logs and later wood, sometimes combined with stone.

It was no easy life for these early settlers. It was a dawn-to-dusk life, one which ranged from plowing to splitting rails and erecting fences around pastures to keep cattle from wandering; cutting cordwood for the home fires; feeding chickens, pigs, and cattle; caring for horses; and repairing not only wagons and harnesses but also everything in the home. A farmer had to be a man of all trades.

Each season had its own requirements. In the spring, the settler plowed the land and sowed the seed. In the summer, he tended to the orchards, cut the winter's supply of cordwood to keep the home warm, and tended the vegetable garden. In the fall, he harvested the crops, took the grain to the mill, and took the apples to the distillery, and in the winter, he cared for the livestock, repaired the house and barns, harvested ice from frozen ponds, and made wood shingles.

Butter and cheese had to be churned, flax grown for making linen and sheep, and hogs and cattle raised and butchered for meat. Women and grown girls dipped candles, made soap, wove carpets, and prepared food for winter storage.

Farmers, who comprised the vast majority of the population and produced the most income, were largely self sufficient, cultivating a variety of crops. Besides hay and grain, they derived a good part of their income from lumbering, grazing, and bee-keeping. On all but the large farms, most of the work was performed by family members. Farmers often exchanged work by sending one or more of their young men to help a neighbor. There were also some bachelors, without much property, who could be hired during the harvest season if extra hands were required.

The more affluent farmers had indentured servants to till the farms, harvest the crops, and care for the animals. There were relatively few slaves.

In response to a petition signed by leading citizens of northern Hunterdon County, the Provincial Legislature in 1739 created Morris County, naming it after Lewis Morris, governor of the province. With the creation of the new county, Morristown became the county seat, mainly because of its central location and the convergence of roads there.

The Court of Common Pleas and General Sessions meeting at Jacob Ford's tavern in Morristown in 1740 created three townships in Morris County, one of which, Morris Township, included the village of Morristown.

After 1750, forges multiplied rapidly. On the Whippany River and its branches in the Morristown area were six or seven forges. One owned by Jacob Ford, one

13

of the most successful of all forge owners, was near Flagler's Mill near Water Street. Two other forges were the Carmichael Forge and the Mackie Forge. Further up the Whippany River at Speedwell was Johnson's Forge. Above that were Hathaway and Ayre's Forges.

In the early days, farm produce was intended mainly for home consumption. Goods that were produced, some at small factories employing only a few people each, were for trading at markets.

Church and tavern, closely allied, were the only two centers for public congregation in Morristown. The town's initial church, the First Presbyterian, an offshoot of the Hanover Presbyterian Church, dates to 1733. A frame building nearly square, it stood on land facing The Green donated by Benjamin Hathaway and Jonathan Lindsley for a parsonage, church, and burial ground. In 1764, a steeple 125 feet tall was added to the building. In its tower was a bell, which tradition says was a gift from the King of England.

When the frame church was replaced in 1774 by a larger edifice to meet the growing needs of its congregation, the steeple was saved and rests today in a corner of the burial ground behind the church. The vane of the steeple was given to the old academy in New Vernon. When the second church was taken down in November 1795, its wood was sold in lots. A good part of it was used to construct a distillery and cider mill in Water Street.

Jacob Ford, who became a leader in Morristown, is credited with bringing Timothy Johnes to town to serve as pastor of the First Presbyterian Church. He served six months of probation, then was named the official pastor of the church, serving until his 93rd birthday, when he preached his last sermon in the old church that had served as a sanctuary, barracks, and hospital for Continental Army soldiers.

His home, on the site of the Mid-Town Shopping Center, became the first Morristown Memorial Hospital in 1893, serving until 1898. The Arnold Tavern, General Washington's headquarters in 1777 and 1778, was moved to Mt. Kemble Avenue and became the first All Soul's Hospital.

The Baptist Church was the second church built in Morristown, by an 11-member congregation formed in 1752, which met for a time in a building 3 miles south of Morristown on Mt. Kemble Avenue. In 1771, a church was built on The Green. Seventy years later, a larger edifice was erected.

Because the cost of relief was considerable, the townships continued the practice of not allowing anyone to enter the township who was likely to become a public charge. Two forms of support for the indigent, home relief and the placement of paupers in private homes, were maintained in the township. From 1768 to 1772, the township raised £100 for poor relief, except in 1768 when it voted only £50. In 1778, with inflation rampant, the figure jumped to £500.

One man, Samuel Ford, marred the reputation that was Morristown's when in 1772, after returning from Ireland where he perfected his trade, he established a counterfeiting plant midway between Morristown and Hanover on an island in a swamp. He would leave his house each morning with his gun as if in pursuit of game and wade through the swamp to the island. Suspicion was aroused and on July 16, 1773, he was arrested and lodged in the county jail.

That night, aided by a confederate, he escaped and sought refuge in the mountains between Mt. Hope and Hibernia before fleeing south to Virginia, paying his way with counterfeit bills and coin. He assumed the name of Baldwin and pursued the trade of a silversmith, marrying his partner's wife although he already had a wife in Hanover and another in Ireland.

At the time of Ford's arrest, several other persons prominent in society were taken into custody. Arraigned in the old courthouse on August 19, 1773, each plead guilty. Sentenced to death, they sought help from influential friends.

As a result, only one was hanged. The others were pardoned. Three of the men confessed that Ford was the prime mover and planner of the robbery of the Treasury of New Jersey at Perth Amboy on July 21, 1768 in which £6,750 and coin were stolen. One admitted he had received £300 of the loot.

For 15 years, court was held and public affairs conducted in Jacob Ford's tavern. Then in 1755, a crude one-story log structure was built near what is now the center of The Green. It served also as a jail until 1770 when the Freeholders purchased from the First Presbyterian Church, owners of The Green, 1 acre on The Green for £5 and erected a one-story shingled structure 35 feet by 45 feet in

*The original First Presbyterian Church was erected c. 1740. The frame structure was razed in 1797 and a larger edifice was constructed.*

*This pen-and-ink sketch is of the Morris County Courthouse in 1776. The building, dating to 1770, was one story until 1776 when a second story and cupola were added.*

size. At the time, a well was dug and a well sweep added to draw water. The pillory and whipping post stood nearby.

In 1776, a second story was added to the courthouse plus a cupola and a bell. A rough-hewn boulder, placed by the Daughters of the American Revolution, marks the site today.

This courthouse and jail served until 1827 when the present brick building in Washington Street was completed. At the time, it was described as one of the handsomest buildings in the state, its interior and exterior being finely finished in the Greco-Roman style.

The cornerstone for the structure, a simple brownstone block containing the date "1827," was formerly laid in ceremonies in July 1826, following a procession from the old courthouse on The Green to the site of the new building two blocks from The Green between Court Street and Western Avenue. In the procession were members of "the grand jury, the gentlemen of the bar, citizens of the town, architects and laborers engaged in construction of the new courthouse."

The land for the new courthouse was purchased by the Freeholders for the sum of $100 from James Wood and his wife. In later years, the courthouse complex was expanded to include first the entire block, then the adjacent block between Court Street and Schuyler Place.

The deed on file in the Hall of Records specifies that, "no part of said premises shall ever be sold or let out for dwelling houses, stores, groceries or workshops for the carrying on of any branch of trade or manufacture whatever." It further provides that the courthouse be erected within five years or the land would revert to James Wood, his heirs, or assigns.

In July 1827, with the courthouse nearing completion, the court appointed a committee to plan dedication ceremonies for the new structure. Henry A. Ford gave the principal address at the dedication ceremonies on September 26, 1827. It followed a procession from The Green and was itself followed by opening of the courts for the September term, and the calling, swearing, and charge to the Grand Jury to sit in the new court edifice.

The procession, which was recreated in part for the observance of the 150th anniversary of the courthouse, included:

> In the following order: 1. music; 2. sheriff; 3. Board of Chosen Freeholders; 4. building committee; 5. master builders; 6. clergy and orator; 7. gaoler and crier; 8. constables; 9. coroners; 10. Justices of the Supreme Court; 11. Judges of the Common Pleas; 12. justices of the peace; 13. clerk and surrogate; 14. attorney general and prosecutor; 15. members of the bar; 16. grand jury; 17. petit jury; 18. collector and assessors; 19 citizens.

It was around and on the historic Morristown Green that many of Morris County's momentous events occurred. On it was built the initial Morris County Courthouse and jail complete with pillory and debtor's room, as well as the Liberty Pole, the Civil War monument, a rustic gazebo for band concerts, and walkways.

During the Civil War, the surrender of Vicksburg and the capture of Richmond occasioned great rejoicing on The Green and in 1865, there was a salute of guns to mark the amendment abolishing slavery. On July 4, 1871, the Soldiers Monument of Quincy granite, surmounted by a soldier boy at rest, was dedicated.

In the beginning, The Green was an open common, "patterned by the homesick New Englanders after the village greens they had known and loved in England." The two-and-a-half acre tract was deeded to the First Presbyterian Church of Morristown in 1758 by Jonathan Lindsley and Benjamin Hathaway. In appearance it was a rough, unkempt piece of land partly covered with oak and walnut trees and with a depression called "the gully" in its center. Animals roamed at will over it.

This forced the First Presbyterian Church, which bordered The Green, to vote "to affix one person" at each door of the meeting house each Sunday to keep stray dogs from entering and distracting the worshippers.

It continued to be owned by the First Presbyterian Church until September 16, 1816 when it was conveyed by the church to 13 civic-minded men, who upon payment of $1,600, became the Trustees of the Morristown Green with the understanding it was to remain "a common forever." A plaque on The Green states the following:

> This Morristown Green was given by the Trustees of the Presbyterian Church in Morristown to the Trustees of the Morristown Green in 1816 to be held in trust for the use and enjoyment of the public and to remain as a common forever.

Here were held fervent meetings of citizens prior to the Revolutionary War protesting taxation, and here Lafayette was welcomed in 1825 when he revisited the scene of the Revolutionary War. Also Antoine LeBlanc was hung here before a crowd of 10,000 for the murder of Samuel Sayre, his wife, and their servant.

LeBlanc was escorted to the gallows on the south side of The Green from the jail by a company of Morris Rangers to the beat of muffled drums. But the crowd, whose vehicles blocked every road into town, brushed the Rangers aside in its rush to get close to the prisoner.

Clustered around The Green were the First Presbyterian, Baptist, and Methodist churches, two of which, the Baptist and Presbyterian, served as smallpox hospitals in the Revolutionary War; also here were Arnold Tavern, General Washington's headquarters in the winter of 1777 and 1778; the Morris County House, a noted hotel (1842); the United States Hotel; and most business and banking establishments.

"No city on earth can purchase the priceless traditions which belong to the few acres of turf and trees that are the common possession of every citizen of Morristown," wrote Reverend William Hughes in 1900 in an appeal to the community for funds to beautify The Green.

The financial condition of the people was far from prosperous, but they were nonetheless zealous in their desire for freedom and desire for the prosecution of the war. While the great mass of the population was Whig, there were also some Tories.

As war fever mounted, The Green became a place for speech making, bonfires, and drills by men and boys of the area. When war came, the courthouse was guarded by a company of soldiers. Prominent Tories and Loyalists from all parts of New Jersey were imprisoned in the jail on The Green, and many important trials were held there. In one, in 1777, 90 persons were tried, 50 of them for treason, with 26 condemned to death.

In Morristown, Jacob Ford was alert and sympathetic to the seething resentment among businessmen and citizens caused by the burden that King George III heaped on the colonists that all iron from the colonies be shipped in pigs to Great Britain to be processed into kettles, hoes, and plows to be reshipped back to America for sale to the colonists.

Before this act of Parliament, colonists had traveled great distances to Morristown to purchase their implements, utensils, and iron-ware from local iron merchants.

*This sketch is of the First Baptist Church, which was built on the northwest corner of The Green in 1771. During the smallpox epidemic of 1777, it and the First Presbyterian Church served as hospitals for Continental Army soldiers.*

In his role as a leader in Morristown, Ford called a meeting June 27, 1774 in which he presided over the drafting and writing of what is possibly one of the first written Declarations of Human Rights in America. It resolved, "the late acts of Parliament for the purpose of raising revenue in America are oppressive and arbitrary, calculated to disturb the minds and alienate the affections of the colonists from the mother country and replete with ruin for both."

It added, "we will most cheerfully join our brethren of other colonies in promoting a union of the colonies by forming a general congress of deputies."

In less than a year, the Province of New Jersey was represented at a meeting in Trenton, whose delegates were selected to meet with those of other colonies in Philadelphia the following year. These delegates formed the first Continental Congress of the United States.

When the Revolutionary War began, Morristown and the region surrounding it were a thriving and somewhat populous farming community, one reason General

Washington chose it for two winter encampments of the Continental Army. From its fields came grain to feed the soldiers, livestock, and wool to be carded, spun, and woven by wives and daughters into fabrics.

Two other reasons existed: the nearness of iron ore mines and forges to turn the raw iron into cannon, cannon balls, and other arms, and New Jersey's only powder-making mill on the Whippany River at Morristown.

Religion had a controlling voice in all the settlers' movements. Sunday was the great day of the week. Pastor Johnes of the First Presbyterian Church could see his congregation coming through the forest from the neighboring farms, riding in wagons or on horseback, the wife behind her husband on the horse. The women were clothed in homespun dresses. In the winter, they brought their footstoves, filled with live coals, to put under their feet during the service. The men disdained such an approach to keeping their feet warm. If there was an evening service, each family brought one or two candles, and persons sat holding them during the meeting, for even candleholders on the walls and pillars of the church were not then provided.

But though the men could bravely sit with cold feet in the winter, they did not hesitate to take off their coats in the heat of the summer. If sleep seemed likely to overpower them during the service, they would stand up until the inclination to drowsiness had passed.

In Morristown's first church, the men sat together on one side of the chapel, with the women and children on the other side of the aisle. The young people occupied the galleries, the young men and boys on one side of the church, the young ladies and girls on the other.

In 1822, woodstoves and lamps were first introduced into the second structure of the First Presbyterian Church at a cost of $254. The action was opposed by a few members of the congregation who held that their mothers and fathers had attended the church without any such comforts, satisfied with the heat of the coals from their foot stoves. The woodstoves were used until 1835 when they were found insufficient for heating the building and coal stoves were substituted. The latter remained in use until furnaces were installed.

# 2. The Revolutionary War Encampments

As 1777 dawned, Sir William Howe, commander in chief of his majesty's army in America, believed the rebellion of Great Britain's colonies crushed beyond hope of revival. The Continental Army had been driven from New York, pursued through New Jersey, and forced to cross the Delaware River into Pennsylvania. Some mopping up might be necessary in the spring, but the hard work of conquest was over.

Then suddenly, with whirlwind effect, these pleasant reveries were swept aside in the roar of American gunfire at Trenton in the cold, gray dawn of December 26, and at Princeton on January 3 by an army one-sixth the size of the British forces.

General Washington had intended to capture New Brunswick and destroy the British stores and magazines there. But the British had heard the cannon at Princeton and as the Americans left Princeton, the van of the British army came in sight. His soldiers exhausted, many having been without sleep for two nights and a day, Washington, heeding the advice of his officers, turned north toward Morristown, the place "best calculated of any in this quarter to accommodate and refresh them."

Unlike present-day wars, the military struggle was marked by six months of active campaigning during the summer and fall and about six months of relative inactivity during the winter and spring. It was this method of campaigning that aided General Washington at Trenton and Princeton. Each winter he would select quarters from which he could watch the British. They, in turn, kept the Continental Army under observation.

The first main encampment of the Continental Army in Morristown on January 6 presented a grim picture. Exhaustion, deplorable health conditions, lack of proper clothing and food, and insufficient pay plagued the soldiers. Many were billeted in private homes, public buildings, barns, and sheds in Morristown and surrounding villages. Others, according to eyewitnesses of the Revolutionary scene, built a village of log huts in the Valley of Loantaka Brook. Snow covered the ground everywhere.

A letter, its writer unknown, dated May 12, 1777 described the Morristown of that day as "a very clever little village, situated in a most beautiful valley at the foot of five mountains." Farming was the mainstay of its people, some 250 in number and largely of New England ancestry. Nearby iron works were already enriching a few families and employing more and more laborers as ore arrived in leather sacks on the backs of horses.

Among the 50 to 60 buildings in Morristown, the more important were the Arnold Tavern, the Presbyterian and Baptist churches, and the Morris County Courthouse and jail, all located on an open green from which streets radiated in several directions. There were also a few sawmills, gristmills, forges, and a powder mill, the latter built on the Whippany River in 1776 by Jacob Ford Jr.

From Morristown, General Washington commanded an extensive agricultural countryside, cutting off its produce from the British and using it instead to feed the Continental Army. In the mountainous region northwest of Morristown were many forges and furnaces, such as those at Hibernia, Mount Hope, Ringwood, and Charlottenburg, from which needed iron supplies were obtained.

The position at Morristown was also difficult for an enemy to attack. Directly eastward, on the main road from Bottle Hill (Madison), large swamp areas guarded the town. Still further east, almost midway between Morristown and the Jersey shore, lay the protecting barriers of Long Hill, and the first and second Watchung Mountain ranges, their parallel ridges stretching out for more than 30 miles, like a huge earthwork, from the Raritan River in the south to the Ramapo Mountains in the north.

*The Arnold Tavern in North Park Place was General George Washington's headquarters in 1777 and 1778. In 1886, it was moved to Mt. Kemble Avenue where it became the first All Soul's Hospital.*

In addition, Morristown was nearly equally distant from Newark, Perth Amboy, and New Brunswick, the main British posts in New Jersey, so that any enemy movement could be met by a counterblow, either from Washington's own outposts or from the center of his defensive web at Morristown.

As an alarm system should the British attempt to attack Morristown, General Washington directed that a series of beacons, manned around the clock by sentinels, be built at intervals along the ridge of the Watchung Mountains. They were made of logs 16 feet square at the base rising to a point with a tar barrel atop a pole. The enclosure formed by the logs was filled with brush. When lit, the fiery beacons could be seen for miles. The most important was built on Prospect Hill, a high point 7 miles east of Morristown.

When the sentinels saw any threatening movement by the British, or news of such movement was brought to them by messengers, an alarm gun was fired or the beacon lit. Immediately, roads were clogged by the militia rushing to the Chatham Bridge prepared to meet the British.

General Washington arrived in Morristown on January 7 and went to the Arnold Tavern on The Green where his headquarters remained throughout the 1777–1778 encampment. The three-story tavern, erected by Jacob Arnold's father around 1750, was a large frame structure with large windows and a veranda in front. Inside, a wide hallway ran from front to rear of the building. On the south side were front and rear parlors. To the right of the entrance on the northern side was the bar room. Back of it was the dining room and kitchen. On the second floor were the bedrooms and ballroom where assemblies were held during the winter. In addition to its social use, the ballroom was the meeting place for the Army Masonic Lodge and the Light Horse Troop of which Jacob Arnold was captain.

While Washington lived at the tavern, he occupied the two bedrooms over the bar room. The front room was used for an office and the rear room for his bedroom. The site is now marked with a State Historic Marker.

Faced with desertions particularly among the volunteer militiamen, many of whom were homesick and most of whom had served beyond their terms of enlistment, General Washington wrote to the President of Congress on January 19: "The fluctuating state of an army, composed chiefly of militia, bids fair to reduce us to the situation in which we were some little time ago, that is, of scarce having an army at all." In another letter several days later, the commander in chief noted his few remaining troops were "absolutely perishing" for want of clothing, "marching over frost and snow, many without a shoe, stocking or blanket."

Congress finally reacted to Washington's pleas for aid, heeding his request for longer enlistments and calling upon the states to raise 88 continental battalions, and also authorizing recruitment of 16 "additional battalions" of infantry, 3,000 light horse, 3 regiments of artillery, and a corps of engineers.

Soon after General Washington's arrival at Morristown, an epidemic of smallpox broke out so severely that it threatened the future of the army. As it ran rampant among the troops at Morristown and broke out in Philadelphia, Washington ordered the first mass inoculation against the disease in American history.

Medical knowledge of that day offered but one real hope of saving the continental forces. That was the inoculation of every soldier who had not yet contracted the disease with a mild form of smallpox to immunize him against its more severe effects.

Washington, informed on the march to Morristown of isolated cases of smallpox that had victimized hundreds of American troops in 1776, was convinced by the time he arrived in Morristown of the need for mass inoculations of the army. He ordered Dr. Nathaniel Bond to proceed without delay to inoculate troops in northern New Jersey and Philadelphia. During the next three months, similar suggestions were sent to officers and civil authorities who were recruiting soldiers in New Jersey, New York, New England, Pennsylvania, and Virginia to fill the quota Congress had authorized.

Undertaken secretly at first, the bold project was soon going full swing throughout Morristown and surrounding villages. Inoculation centers were established in private homes, with guards around each to prevent the spread of the infection. As of March 4, 1777, about 1,000 soldiers and their attendants were still incapacitated in Morristown, leaving only 2,000 others as the army's total effective strength in northern New Jersey. The episode was not without its tragic side, however. Since smallpox was highly contagious, civilians in the countryside near the camps also had to be inoculated. Some local residents contracted the disease before the project got underway or refused to submit to the treatment.

Isolation hospitals were established in the Baptist and Presbyterian churches in Morristown, in homes, and in the Presbyterian Church in Hanover. Nevertheless, scores of civilians and soldiers alike died. In the congregation of the First Presbyterian Church, for example, 68 civilian deaths were recorded before the plague was contained in September 1777. Those who survived were almost always pockmarked.

Besides the safety afforded by the protecting mountain ranges, one of the reasons for General Washington choosing Morristown for his winter encampment in 1777 and 1778 may have been to protect an important powder mill on the Whippany River.

As the war progressed, an acute shortage of gunpowder developed. To solve the problem, Jacob Ford "offered to erect a powder mill in the County of Morris for the making of gunpowder." The Provincial Congress agreed to lend him £2,000, without interest, on his giving "satisfactory security for the same to be repaid within the time of one year in good merchantable powder," the first installment of "one ton of powder" to be paid "on first of July next, and one ton per month thereafter til the sum of 2,000 English pounds be paid."

Soon a powder mill (the only one in New Jersey), salt peter, and ash houses were constructed on the Whippany River near Jacob Ford's new home. All who had salt peter, a major ingredient in gunpowder, for sale were asked to bring it to the mill, where a price of four shillings, two pence a pound was paid.

"On occasion," it was reported, "when powder with the army was low," Captain Benoni Hathaway, who operated the mill, "filled barrels with sand and carted them to the magazine to hoodwink spies and Tories into thinking that the mill was producing a huge amount of gunpowder."

This powder, used by the Continental Army in many battles, is thought to be one of the main reasons for the repeated but fruitless attempts of the British to reach Morristown. The first attempt made in December 1776, only a few months after the powder mill started operation, was rebuffed by Ford and 700 militia at Springfield.

The exact location of the site of the two-story frame powder mill powered by a large water wheel remains a mystery. Research shows the building was moved 100 feet to a meadow in the rear of the Lindsley farm house in 1815, 16 years after an advertisement appeared in the *Genius of Liberty* offering for sale a powder mill with any quantity of land adjoining from 1 to 10 acres. The advertisement was placed by Joseph Lindsley Sr.

Archeological research and diggings uncovered what seemed to be a first floor of fieldstone, including a number of bricks believed to be the floor of a stamping mill associated with the powder mill. It was on the river bank in the rear of what is now the Westin Hotel on the Whippany Road.

To defend Morristown, General Washington ordered a fort to be built on Kinney's Hill rising 230 feet above the village green to protect the army stores kept in Morristown, many in the two-story continental storehouse, afterwards O'Hara's Tavern, facing The Green where Epstein's Department Store is today. The reconstructed earthworks at Fort Nonsense, which was built in the on Kinney's Hill overlooking Morristown in 1777, was a retreat "in case of necessity" for troops assigned to guard United States military stores.

How the name "Fort Nonsense" came into being is unknown. It does not appear in any written record before 1833, nor has anyone authenticated the oft-

*The Ford powder mill on the Whippany River, built by Colonel Jacob Ford Jr. in 1776, supplied powder for the Continental Army. It was the only powder mill in New Jersey.*

*The reconstructed earthworks at Fort Nonsense were built on Kinney's Hill, overlooking Morristown in 1777, as a retreat "in case of necessity" for troops assigned to guard American military stores.*

repeated tale that Washington's reasons for constructing it were merely to keep the United States troops occupied and out of mischief.

His real reason, however, is disclosed by an order issued as the Continental Army moved south to Middlebrook. In this, he directed Lieutenant Colonel Jeremiah Olney to remain behind at Morristown and, with his detachment:

> strengthen the earthworks already begun upon the hill and erect such others as are necessary for the better defending of it, that it may become a safe retreat in case of necessity. The guard house in the upper redoubt should be immediately finished and if you are not able to mount a guard in it, at present, you should make it the quarters of a trusty sergeant and select party of men. Otherwise, if the enemy or their Tory assistants should have any designs upon the town or the public stores in it their first attempt will be to seize the height and turn our own works against us.

As years passed, the original line of earthworks, marked only by a marker erected by the Washington Association of New Jersey, gradually crumbled. A bronze plaque mounted on a large stone states: "This stone marks the site of Fort Nonsense, an earthwork built by the Continental Army in the winter of 1779-80."

In 1937, the National Park Service, following extensive research, restored the earthworks to their original appearance and built an approach road, parking area, restrooms, and documentary displays at the 53-acre site. Vandals and lack of sufficient maintenance funds sounded the death knell for the restoration, most of which was either destroyed by vandalism or demolished by park officials as a safety measure prior to the closing of the area in the mid-1950s.

In 1959, the National Park Service sought to reopen the fort site, but lacked the necessary funds to immediately finance the project. Morristown's town fathers, who held the purse strings on a $69,215 trust fund that "could be used" for the redevelopment, were hindered by red tape that would require an act of Congress and court action to untangle.

Efforts to use the fund, bequeathed by the estate of Francis E. Woodruff, one-time honorary president of the Fort Nonsense Association and one of the few American citizens to become a mandarin of China, had failed once. Park Service spokesmen said funds to restore the fort were included in Mission 66, a nationwide program to update national parks. It was not known, however, when they would be appropriated.

The fort, reconstructed for a second time in the 1960s, has once again fallen into a state of disrepair; its earthworks, flagpole, cannon platforms, and vista paths, slashed through trees to provide views of Morristown, have all but disappeared.

The first official celebration of the Declaration of Independence was held in Morristown by order of General Washington on July 4, 1777. He announced "that this, the first anniversary of the Declaration of Independence, should be celebrated by a Fue-de-Joie and that every soldier should be issued an extra gill of rum."

It was during his residence at the Arnold Tavern in 1777 that Washington joined Reverend Timothy Johnes in the Presbyterian Church's semi-annual communion after receiving the minister's assurances "ours is not the Presbyterian Table but the Lord's Table, and we give the Lord's invitation to all his followers of whatever name." This is said to be the only occasion that Washington partook of the Sacrament. The event took place in an apple orchard behind Reverend Johnes's house because the church had become a smallpox hospital.

By the time the snow melted and buds appeared on the trees in the spring of 1780, prospects spurred by Congressional action and increased recruitment had brightened. General Washington had in New Jersey a total of 8,188 men, the enlistments being for either three years or until the war was over. There was an abundance of arms and ammunition, including 1,000 barrels of powder, 11,000 gun flints, and 22,000 muskets sent from France.

Uneasy because of British movements, General Washington decided to leave Morristown on May 28, leaving a small detachment to guard military stores in the village and moving the Continental Army south to Middlebrook Valley from where he could both defy attack and threaten any overland expedition the enemy might make.

Nearly two-and-a-half years passed before the main body of the Continental Army, numbering between 10,000 and 12,000 men, returned to Morristown in early December 1779 and established camp 3 miles south of the village in Jockey Hollow on farms owned by Peter Kemble, Henry Wick, and Joshua Guerin.

General Washington arrived on December 1 and established his headquarters at the Ford mansion.

For nearly seven months in 1779 and 1780, Morristown was the military headquarters of the American Revolution. The center of this capital was the home of Theodosia Ford and her children. For that period, she was hostess not only to General and Mrs. Washington, but to 15 members of his military staff.

It may be said that within the walls of this old headquarters building gathered more famous persons connected with the War for Independence than ever assembled under one roof in America. Included were generals, statesmen, foreign envoys, and members of Congress.

The soldiers arriving at Jockey Hollow pitched their tents on the frozen ground, then began building log huts, cutting down 600 acres of oak, walnut, and chestnut trees. Washington ordered all the huts to be alike, lined up neatly in rows with the soldiers in front and officers behind. They housed 12 men each and were arrayed in groups of two in rows across hillsides with a 12-foot by 20-foot lane between the rows.

The Pennsylvania Brigade, the First and Second Maryland, First and Second Connecticut, Stark's, Hand's, New York, and New Jersey Brigades constructed an estimated 1,000 huts over an area that is now part of Mendham, Harding, and Morris Townships and Bernardsville. Knox's four artillery regiments, field pieces, heavy guns, forges, and machine shops were located about a mile west of Morristown on the main road to Mendham where the artillery park was established, almost opposite Burnham Park.

The site is marked today by a 5-foot-tall boulder, benches, and a flag pole. A bronze plaque mounted on the boulder reads:

> The Artillery Park. The artillery under Gen. Henry Knox and the artipicers [artificers] under Col. Jeduthran Baldwin were encamped on this hillside during 1779-80. The soldiers were housed in huts. The guns were parked along this road. The horses were pastured in what is now Burnham Park. Erected by Morristown Post No. 59, American Legion, November 11, 1932.

On the opposite side of the lake, once a pasture, stood a replica of a soldiers' hut used by ice skaters in the winter months to keep warm. A chimney is all that now remains. A plaque on it gives a broad overview of the army in Morristown. It reads:

> Continental Army Encampment. 1779–1780. Brig. Gen. Henry Knox in command of the artillery of the Continental Army used this field now covered by these ponds as pasture for the artillery horses. His soldiers lived in log huts erected on the hillside to the west. Nine brigades of the Continental Army were hutted in Jockey Hollow. Gen. Washington occupied the Ford mansion on Morris Avenue. The troops were in Morristown from December 1, 1779 to June 23, 1780.

*A British war map shows the position of General Washington's Continental Army encampment at Jockey Hollow in 1780. Shown are Washington's headquarters, the position of the brigades in Jockey Hollow, the roads to Chatham and Basking Ridge, and the mountains protecting Morristown.*

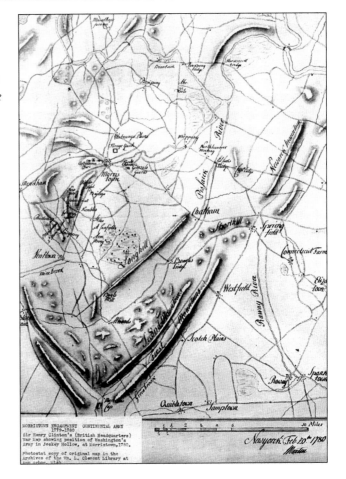

Each brigade camped in Jockey Hollow occupied a sloping, well-drained area about 320 yards long and 100 yards deep, including a parade ground 40 yards deep in front of the huts. Logs notched together at the corners and chinked with clay formed the sides of the huts. Boards, slabs, or hand-split shingles covered the simple gable roofs, the ridges of which ran parallel to the camp streets. Each soldiers' hut was 14 feet wide, 15 to 16 feet long, and 6.5 feet high at the eaves. They were equipped with wooden bunks, a fireplace and chimney at one end, and a door in the front side. Windows were added in the spring.

The officers' huts were larger in size, usually accommodating two to four officers. They had two fireplaces and chimneys and frequently two or more doors and windows.

A focal point of the sprawling "log cabin city" at Jockey Hollow was the Grand Parade Ground. Each day, guard details assembled on it for inspection, general orders from Washington's headquarters, and a short drill. This was also the site of formal military reviews, and the place where those guilty of serious crimes were executed and buried.

The original parade ground was 400 yards long and 100 yards wide, six times the size of the clearing that marks its place today. The camp guard, composed of 27 men from every two regiments, surrounded Jockey Hollow with a chain of sentinels.

All of the brigade locations are shown on excellent maps of the period prepared by Robert Erskine, Washington's geographer general, and Captain Bichet Rochefontaine, a French engineer.

The original huts stood in place until the war's end. Then local residents dismantled them to reuse the logs, hardware, and shingles in part as compensation for the vast amount of timber cut from their forests to make and heat the huts.

Weather conditions when the army arrived in Morristown were only a taste of what was to come. The elements attacked the army before all the huts were constructed. The worst snowstorm was the great blizzard of January 2–4, 1780, described as among the most memorable on record. A Dr. Thacher wrote: "Some of the soldier's were actually covered while in their tents and buried like sheep under the snow." When the blizzard subsided, snow lay 4 feet deep, drifting in places to 6 feet. It filled the roads, covered the tops of fences, and made travel almost impossible during much of January and February. One soldier wrote after his arrival at camp:

> It was cold and snowy. We had to march all day through the snow and at
> night take up our lodgings in some wood, where, after shoveling away

*This reconstructed typical log hut was used by the officers and soldiers in the winter encampment at Jockey Hollow from 1779 to 1780. To construct more than 1,000 huts, 600 acres of trees were felled.*

the snow, we used to pitch three or four tents facing each other, and then join in making a fire in the center. Sometimes we could procure an armful of buckwheat straw to lie upon, which was indeed a luxury. Provisions, as usual, took up but a small part of our time, though much of our thoughts.

One observer recorded four snows in November, seven in December, six in January, four in February, six in March, and one in April. What made things worse was the intense bone-chilling cold. "The oldest people now living in the county," wrote General Washington on March 18, "do not remember so hard a winter as the one we are now emerging from."

Washington was having his troubles at his headquarters. He wrote to General Nathanial Green, the army's quartermaster general, that nothing had been done to improve the accommodations at the Ford mansion:

> I have been at my present quarters since the 1st day of December and I have not a kitchen to cook a dinner in, altho the logs have been put together some considerable time by my own guard; nor is there a place at the moment in which a servant can lodge with the smallest degree of comfort.

In addition, he added, 18 of his aides were crowded together in Mrs. Ford's kitchen, all with colds so bad that scarcely one of them could speak above a whisper.

General Green soon had a log kitchen constructed at the east end of the Ford mansion. He also had an office built at the west end of the house. Both were razed after the war. Fourteen log huts were built opposite the Ford house for Washington's guard of 250 men. A life-size statue of General Washington astride his horse stands today at the approximate location of these huts at the intersection of Morris Street and Washington Avenue. The statue was donated to Morristown in 1927 by Miss Ella Mabel Clark, daughter of Charles Finny Clark, president of New York's Bradstreet Company. The sculptor was Frederick G.R. Roth.

Whenever an alarm was sounded, the lifeguard would immediately rush to the Ford mansion, barricade the doors, and throw up the windows. Five soldiers with their muskets cocked were placed at each window where they remained until troops arrived or the cause of the alarm was ascertained.

Erskine's map of Morristown shows the exact location of 13 or 14 huts built by the guard unit, most members of which were from Virginia, for winter quarters. Except for minor changes introduced after March 1779, the guard uniform included a dark blue coat with buff collar and facings, red vest, fitted buckskin breeches, black shoes, white bayonet and body belts, black stock and tie for the hair, and black cocked hat bound with white tape. The buttons were gilt.

The trial of Major General Benedict Arnold, an event that drew much attention at Morristown during the winter of 1780, opened in the Dickerson Tavern on

December 23 and continued through Christmas Day, lasting until late in January when he was acquitted on all except two minor charges on grounds of insufficient evidence. He was charged with consorting with the enemy in 1778 while in command at Philadelphia. General Washington reprimanded Arnold in general orders in response to the recommendation of the court. Only a year-and-a-half later, he would be shocked to learn of Arnold's treason at West Point.

Romance flourished amid the 1779–1780 encampment. Elizabeth Schuyler, a "brunette with the most good natured lively dark eyes" came to Morristown late in 1779 to visit her aunt, the wife of Dr. John Cochran who lived with Dr. Jabez Campfield, General Washington's personal physician, on the road between the Ford mansion and the village green. Alexander Hamilton, one of Washington's aides, met her while delivering papers to the doctor, and became infatuated with her. After a whirlwind romance, the couple were married in December 1779 at General Schuyler's house in Albany.

The Cochran house, since moved to 5 Olyphant Place, is on the list of Morris County's 10 most threatened historic sites for the second year. Now a museum, it has been maintained by the Daughters of the American Revolution since 1923. The list is compiled annually by four groups: the Morris County Heritage Commission, the Morris County Historical Society, the Morris County Trust for Historic Preservation, and the Morris County Visitors Center.

In 1780, funds were sought for a subscription dance to be held at O'Hara's Tavern on The Green. The notice announcing the dance and seeking funds to finance it read: "The subscribers agree to pay the sums annexed to their respective names and an equal quota of any further expense which may be incurred in the promotion and support of a dancing assembly to be held in Morristown the present winter of 1780." A total of $13,600 was subscribed by 29 officers and General Washington.

Great difficulty was experienced in the spring of 1780 in obtaining horses, both for the calvary and to move the army stores from Morristown. Tempe Wick, 22-year-old daughter of Henry Wick, on whose 1,000-acre farm many of the Continental Army soldiers were encamped, was riding a young horse home from visiting her sister Phoebe, wife of Dr. William Leddell, who resided on the Mendham Road, when she was stopped by a party of soldiers intent on taking her horse. She appeared to submit to their demands but not before telling them she was sorry to part with the horse and asked they return him if possible and treat him well.

The soldiers, assuming she was about to dismount, dropped the reins they had grabbed. She touched the horse with her whip and rode at high speed to the Wick farmhouse where she led the animal into a small room. The soldiers, who had fired, but missed as she fled, approached the house and searched the barns and woods in vein. She kept the horse in the house for three weeks until the last troops had left the area.

The shingled farmhouse, later part of the 4,000-acre estate of Luther Kountze, millionaire New York banker, was donated to the park by Lloyd W. Smith, who bought it from another party. The barns and outbuildings, termed unsafe, were razed by the National Park Service in 1951. The house was the headquarters of Major General Arthur St. Clair in the winter of 1779–1780.

The Wick House was restored in 1935 by the Park Service and its farm garden, orchard, and smoke house in 1936. The barns believed to have been the original barns for the Wick House were also reconstructed that year. The outbuildings, including the pig sty, sheep barn, and cow shed, were destroyed by fire in 1957.

The Wick House early furnishings, many of which are in the house today, included a weaving loom, a brass kettle, pots, kettles, andirons, several pails, a pair of tongs, girdling irons, pewter dishes, spinning wheels, milk room furniture, three beds and bedding, a case with drawers, a desk, four chests, four tables and nine chairs, a looking glass, one watch, one gun, old casks, nine barrels of cider, and one barrel of whiskey.

On May 10, 1780, following more than a year's absence in his native France, the Marquis de Lafayette brought word to General Washington at headquarters in Morristown that King Louis XVI was sending a second major fleet of ships and men to aid the Americans. This assistance proved more beneficial than the first French expedition, which after failing to capture Newport in the late summer of 1778, sailed away to the West Indies.

On June 21, 1780, General Washington, learning of a British invasion of New Jersey and the capture of General Lincoln and his army of 5,000 Continental soldiers at Charleston, South Carolina, decided it was time to abandon Morristown as his main base of operations. After a battle at Springfield and

*The Wick House in Jockey Hollow was occupied by Major General Arthur St. Clair in the winter of 1779 and 1780. It became famous as the house in which Tempe Wick hid her horse from soldiers.*

*This diorama scene shows General Anthony Wayne endeavoring to halt the Pennsylvania mutineers, who were marching to Philadelphia to lay their case before Congress.*

assurances that the British had retired to Staten Island, he marched his army north to the Hudson Highlands.

In January 1781, when most of Washington's army was encamped north of West Point, the Pennsylvania Line, consisting of ten infantry regiments and one of artillery, occupied the log huts built at Jockey Hollow the previous winter. Morale was extremely low. Not only did the Pennsylvanians lack clothing and blankets, but they were without rum to fortify themselves against the freezing cold and had not been paid in 12 months.

Major General Anthony Wayne, their commander, had known for a long time that trouble was brewing and had repeatedly urged the authorities of his state to act. His entreaties fell on deaf ears. Tired of pleading, the men as a last resort turned to mutiny. On New Year's Day, 1781, they seized the ammunition and artillery and prepared to leave camp.

Captain Adam Bettin was killed and two others wounded attempting to stop their march to Philadelphia to carry their case direct to Congress. Bettin was buried by a towering black oak tree by the side of the Jockey Hollow Road overlooking the Wick orchard and farmhouse. A monument erected by the Morristown Chapter of the DAR at the site reads: "In memory of Capt. Adam Bettin shot in the mutiny of January 1, 1781." It replaced an earlier monument erected by the DAR, the present location of which is a mystery. Congress and Pennsylvania authorities successfully negotiated the soldiers' issue at Princeton where the mutineers had stopped after General Wayne's endeavors to end the mutiny. In an effort to save the 200-year-old 70-foot-high tree, extensive tree surgery was authorized on December 18, 1933. A split near its top had permitted rain water to reach the heart of the trunk and rot it. The tree has since been taken down.

Native Morristonians began to grow history-conscious in the autumn of 1929 when an elaborate observance of the sesquicentennial of the Revolutionary cantonment was held. Three years later, a remarkable pageant in commemoration of the Washington bicentennial was staged before thousands of spectators.

Clyde Potts, Morristown's mayor for 24 years (1921–1934) and an internationally renowned sanitary engineer, might well be termed the "father" of Morristown National Historical Park, the first such park established in the nation by the National Park Service.

When Potts formed his dream to perpetuate the many historical sites in and around Morristown into plans in the late 1920s and early 1930s, the area now comprising the Morristown National Historical Park was valuable real estate in the possession of many owners. The major section of Jockey Hollow had recently been purchased by a group of men who realized its potential real estate value. In addition to these areas, Morristown owned about 100 acres in the Jockey Hollow area.

Without the aid of Morristown's millionaires of the "Gilded Age," Potts's dream might never have materialized. To acquire this valuable property seemed beyond the realm of Alladin's wildest dream. Potts and several citizens called upon Lloyd W. Smith of Florham Park, a philanthropist, for assistance. He became chairman of a committee including Colonel Franklin D'Olier; Charles W. Parker, a Morris County judge; Miss Ella Mabel Clark, daughter of Charles Finny Clark, president of New York's Bradstreet Company; William P. Jenks, senior member of the New York Stock Exchange firm of Jenks, Gwynne and Company; Mrs. Mildred Ennis; and William H. Dutton.

The committee sought to acquire all property in and around Jockey Hollow having historical significance. Its initial report made one year later revealed that Smith had purchased more than 800 acres from the Sahagi Realty Corporation, plus several hundred acres from Mrs. Austin Brady. Shortly thereafter, Charles W. McAlpin, a capitalist who during his lifetime collected one of the best known complete series of Washington engravings and prints in the country, donated 125 acres adjacent to the property purchased by Smith. Altogether, the holdings totaled 1,051 acres. Smith told the following to the committee:

> as has already appeared in the public press, a very large part of the sites of Revolutionary interest in Jockey Hollow, other than those owned by Morristown, have been acquired and purchase of certain other sites of historic interest are under discussion to become a part of the park. As soon as these discussions have been concluded and after completion of maps and surveys this area should be offered to the Federal Government for a National Park in commemoration of our patriotic forefathers who encamped and suffered there during the winter of 1779–1780.

In November 1920, Morristown residents held a referendum under a special act of the New Jersey Legislature and voted to donate the Morristown-owned property to the federal government. Included was the property comprising Fort Nonsense and other tracts which earlier had been bequeathed to the town by Francis Woodruff.

Potts immediately opened negotiations with the government to accept the historical tract as a perpetual national historical site maintained by the federal government. After investigation supported Potts's dream that Jockey Hollow constituted a national shrine, the government agreed to accept the site from the Washington Association of New Jersey, Morristown, and Smith, and maintain it forever as the nation's first National Historical Park. Among the last acts of Herbert Hoover as president was the signing on March 2, 1933 of legislation approved by Congress to create the park.

On May 25, 1933, 25 men, the advance guard of 200 workers, federal surveyors, laborers, and army officers, arrived at Jockey Hollow to establish a reforestation camp and begin work on the creation of the new national park.

In 1936, the Civilian Conservation Corps (CCC) provided the newly designated park with resources for an archeological survey of the Pennsylvania Line. By 1940, an officers' log hut was recreated incorporating an original hearth. This hut was razed in 1964 when it started to topple over. The CCC built a total of five huts on the Pennsylvania Line between 1964 and 1966 after an archeological survey to discover if additional hut traces existed to avoid placement of huts on original sites.

On June 28, 1933, Horace M. Albright, director of the National Park Service, outlined the importance of the Morristown National Historical Park: "Morristown more than any other place during that period is the key to the study not only to the military movements of the Revolutionary War, but also of its political and economic aspects."

On August 16, 1933, Smith announced that $578,000 would be sought from the federal government: $400,000 for erection of a museum and $178,000 for construction of a scenic boulevard from Fort Nonsense to Jockey Hollow. Plans for the boulevard provided for a 90-foot-wide road punctuated with parkway greens. It was, he said, to be the main entrance to the park. Smith owned the right of way along most of the proposed route and signified his intention of donating a strip 140 feet wide for the new boulevard. Unfortunately, inability to obtain a right of way on several parcels of land doomed the venture.

A military hospital, one of three Revolutionary War buildings reconstructed in 1958 after extensive historical and archeological research, replaced a similar building constructed by the Works Progress Administration (WPA) and CCC in 1934. The original hospital was razed in the mid-1950s as unsafe for public inspection after it started to collapse.

While outwardly faithful in appearance to its Revolutionary War prototype, the reconstructed hospital differed slightly from the 22-year-old replica it replaced. The one-story log walls and split cedar shingles were treated with a wood preservative to ward off decay, a major factor in the old building's collapse; a

*This army hospital in Jockey Hollow was reconstructed by the National Park Service from plans prepared by Dr. James Tilton, hospital physician in 1779 and 1780. It was razed by the Park Service because they could find no evidence it existed where it was located.*

cement floor was added; land around the hospital was graded to improve drainage; and brush was removed. The latter was cheered by camera fans, many of whom had climbed trees to obtain an unobstructed view of the hospital building.

The reconstructed hospital was based on plans prepared by Dr. James Tilton, hospital surgeon at Morristown in 1779 and 1780, and later physician and surgeon general of the Army. Measuring 66 feet by 34 feet, the Revolutionary War structure had a central ward and two wings crudely built of large oak logs chinked with mud and straw and roofed with hand-split cedar shingles. Heat was provided by stone fireplaces in each ward. A major attraction at the park for years, the hospital no longer exists. Park officials ordered it razed and an outdoor pictorial and text exhibit removed, on the basis that archeological diggings did not confirm the hospital existed where it was located but was probably south of Bernardsville. No further action has been taken on locating its site.

Behind the hospital in a grove of 30-foot tall cedar trees is the burying ground where more than 100 soldiers lie. A plaque on a large boulder dedicated May 30, 1932 reads:

> Jockey Hollow Cemetery. More than 100 Continental soldiers who made the supreme sacrifice for American liberty are buried in this cemetery. Their comrades were housed in huts along the Jockey Hollow Road. The people of Morristown reverently erect this monument as a tribute to them and to the valor of the army whose occupancy of Jockey Hollow has hallowed this ground.

Originally, a chain link fence strung between 4-foot-high posts painted white surrounded the cemetery. The graves were marked by a grove of locust trees, long since cut down.

Today, the huts of the Pennsylvania Line, again in need of rehabilitation, are receiving some work. The grading around the huts has been improved to prevent moisture damage, rotted logs have been replaced, and the chinking between the logs renewed and the roofs repaired. The work is made possible by the National Park Service recreational fee demonstration program, which allows 80 percent of entrance fees to be retained for such projects. Started in 1999, the project is conducted under a cooperative agreement between the National Park Service, the Washington Association of New Jersey, and volunteer support.

Located throughout the 1,500 acres of Jockey Hollow at huts, the Grand Parade Ground, Old Camp Road, the Wick House, and individual brigade camp sites, are descriptive signs and large billboard-type displays with maps and illustrations prepared by the National Park Service relating the story of major points of interest.

When the population of Jockey Hollow jumped from two or three farmers to 10,000 soldiers, the army had to build some roads. In 1933, it cost $200,000 to reconstruct them. Typical is the Old Camp Road, which ran between two pre-Revolutionary era roads, the Jockey Hollow Road and the Basking Ridge Road (Route 202), and the site of Jacob Larzeleer's tavern where General Stark made his quarters in 1779 and 1780. Part of the road may have been built originally as the result of orders issued to Stark's and the New York brigades on April 25, 1780 to "open a road between the two encampments."

In 1872, the Ford mansion, General Washington's headquarters, and its contents were advertised for sale at auction. The last of the Ford family to occupy the mansion had died. The auction attracted the attention of Theodore F. Randolph, New Jersey governor (1869–1872); Edmund D. Halsey; General

*The Ford Mansion, built on Morris Street, was selected for General Washington's headquarters in 1779 and 1780 because it would present an image impressive to visitors, both foreign and domestic.*

N.N. Halstead; and William V. Lidgerwood, an industrialist. These men attended the auction and purchased the mansion, which included Washington's rooms and furniture, for $25,000. They then petitioned the state legislature for a charter to place the property in perpetuity under state maintenance. To supervise and preserve the mansion, they formed the Washington Association of New Jersey in 1874, officered by these men who maintained the property for 59 years. For much of this period, Jonathan W. Roberts, a New York dry goods merchant and president of the association, collected many relics of the Revolution, including more personal belongings of Washington than are to be found anywhere except at Mount Vernon.

The Ford mansion, located approximately one half-mile from The Green, was the handsomest private residence in Morristown for many years. The main portion was two stories high. Four rooms entered off a center hall on the first floor and an equal number on the second floor. A wing, also two stories high, contained servants' rooms, a pantry, and kitchen. The residence was built of brick with an exterior finish of wood.

The choice of the Ford mansion for Washington's headquarters was based on several factors. They included the comfort of Washington and his wife Martha, who joined him in December 1779; adequate quarters for his military staff of 10 to 15 officers; and a headquarters that would present an image impressive to visitors, both foreign and domestic.

The office of the aides was on the west side of the hall on the first floor. Here and in the log structure Washington had built west of the mansion for office purposes, correspondence to and from headquarters was drafted and answered.

Immediately after the arrival of Mrs. Washington, some of the principal ladies of Morristown made a formal visit to welcome her to their society. Dressed in their most elegant gowns and wearing their jewels, they were ushered into the presence of Mrs. Washington, by whom they were cordially received. They were surprised, however, to find her dressed in a very plain gown of homespun linen. A white kerchief covered her neck and bosom. She wore a neat cap and no ornament but a gold wedding ring. With her right hand she gave each a friendly greeting. In her left hand she held a half-knit stocking, one of many she knitted for the troops. They were more surprised to observe her, while engaged in conversation, ply her knitting needles incessantly.

The mansion was first used by the army in 1777 as quarters for a brief period for the Delaware Light Infantry Regiment commanded by Captain Thomas Rodney. During the encampment of 1779–1780, all but two rooms in the residence were occupied by Washington's official family, which besides the general himself included his wife, Martha; his aides-de-camp; and some servants.

The mansion, overlooking Morristown, was built by Colonel Jacob Ford Jr., an influential citizen, iron manufacturer, powder mill owner, and soldier. He died January 10, 1777 from an illness contracted during the campaign of 1776 when he served as commander of the Eastern Battalion, Morris County Militia. He was buried with military honors in the graveyard of the First Presbyterian Church.

# 3. FROM HORSE AND BUGGY TO AUTOMOBILE

The emergence of the 1800s witnessed a dramatic transition in Morristown's development, both socially, economically, and industrially, a transition that was to rocket man to new heights of expansion and means of accomplishing new goals. Inventiveness, developing industry, and expansion were the order of the day.

It was an era of scintillating progress. Science and invention were producing fresh miracles almost daily, moving the infant nation into and through the industrial age to undreamt of heights in the dawn of the twentieth century. The story of this progress is a colorful saga, infused with dreams and daring, wickedness and guile, goodness and gaiety. It sparkles with accomplishments, crackles with excitement, and is crisscrossed with a pattern of dramatic events.

The gleam, pathos, and hardships of the Revolutionary War were over. Morristown soldiers came home to pursue peace-time challenges, which, with the casting aside of Great Britain's yoke opened up possibilities never before experienced.

Samuel F.B. Morse and Alfred Vail Jr. sent the first message over the electro-magnetic telegraph at Speedwell; the railroad came to Morristown; the Morris Canal conceived by George F. Macculloch, a Morristown millionaire, was completed across the state; the historic Morris County Courthouse was built; the machinery for the *Savannah*, the first ship to cross the Atlantic Ocean under steam power, was built at the Speedwell Iron Works; All Soul's and Memorial Hospitals opened their doors; turnpikes fanned out from Morristown in four directions; and Morristown's first public school was built.

Life was simpler then. Horses and carriages rolled around The Green, their drivers alert for empty hitching posts; the scissors grinder attracted groups of small boys, who watched in awe as he put an edge on cutlery; gas lamps and later electric light bulbs provided illumination; and the woman of the house, a shopping basket over her arm, walked to market.

As the nineteenth century dawned, streets were still dirt, the first public library was established, and the first newspaper, the *Morris County Gazette*, was published, followed a year later by the *Genius of Liberty*. Lafayette, the French hero of the

40

American Revolution, returned to view the encampment sites and headquarters; new churches, hotels, office buildings, and stores were erected; and the first women's college in New Jersey opened in Convent.

Speedwell Avenue, Market and South Streets, all dotted with stores and houses, vied with The Green as the core of the business district. Scattered on the district's fringes were the giant ice houses in which ice cut from ponds was stored for summertime use, the stables where horses were kept for hotel patrons, and the railroad stations, freight yards, and huge piles of coal the steam engines consumed.

Food prices at the dusk of the eighteenth century were different, too. Milk was 14¢ a quart; three-quarters of a pound of haddock, 50¢; butter, 55¢ a pound; beef liver, 15¢ a pound; ground hamburger meat, 25¢ a pound; 1.5 pounds of roundsteak, 48¢ ; coffee rings, 12¢; and homemade bread, 10¢ a loaf.

For the well-to-do, shopping was a delightful experience. Most stores had bells attached to posts outside the store. The coachmen rang them with the butts of their whips to summon clerks to the waiting carriages, whether to pick up an order or request a chocolate soda and chicken sandwich.

Some provisions came to the doorsteps of the spacious, well maintained houses of prosperous townspeople just off The Green, each surrounded by trim lawns, striped awnings, flowering shrubbery, and spreading shade trees.

Cries of "sweet, ripe strawberries, 10¢ a quart; new June peas, fresh, crisp lettuce, new potatoes, and eggs, 12¢ a dozen," heralded the arrival of the produce vendor's wagon.

*This barn at Speedwell Iron Works is where Samuel F.B. Morse and Alfred Vail perfected the telegraph in 1838 and sent the first message, "a patient waiter is no loser."*

*This picture is a sketch of Speedwell Lake c. 1890. The side wheel steamboat that made excursions on the lake is visible between the island and the shore.*

Townspeople rarely traveled to Newark or New York to shop. Instead they shopped locally, purchasing ready made hats at Dudgeon and Company; carriages, wagons, harnesses, and horse furnishings from John H. Schmitt; writing paper, calling cards, and school supplies from Emmell's Stationery; and imported table delicacies from Acker, Merrill & Condit.

Black and white movies, or flicks as some people called them, came to Morristown in the dusk of the nineteenth century, vying with the minstrel shows and the circus for popularity, not only locally but in towns for miles around. Stores closed and schools let out early so clerks and children could watch the parades from the railroad yards to The Green, where for many years the circuses were held. Later, they moved to fields on South Street.

## THE TELEGRAPH AND SPEEDWELL VILLAGE

A ministerial student, a professor of fine arts, and an industrialist: this was the unlikely trio that set out in the 1830s at Morristown to prove that something called the telegraph could actually be made to work.

Alfred Vail was the student. He met Professor Samuel F.B. Morse, the artist-inventor, at a demonstration of Morse's crude new telegraph at New York University in 1837. Young Vail was enthusiastic. He persuaded his father Judge Stephen Vail to lend the pair $2,000 and the use of his Speedwell Iron Works for experiments. Then, while Morse painted portraits of Judge and Mrs. Vail, Alfred went to work to eliminate the bugs in the telegraph equipment.

On January 6, 1838, Morse and Vail invited the judge to "come down and see the telegraph machine work." The judge wrote out a message "A patient waiter is no loser." Alfred started sending the message through 3 miles of cotton-covered copper wire strung around the factory barn. The judge wrote in his diary: "They have worked the telegraph in the factory this evening for the first time." In celebration, he invited everyone from neighboring communities to a demonstration of the new invention and an oyster dinner.

Successful demonstrations followed in New York, Philadelphia, and Washington. It was Vail who changed Morse's cumbersome code into simple dots and dashes, the same dots and dashes used in the historic first public message between Washington and Baltimore in 1844—"What hath God wrought?"

Speedwell Village preserves part of the 1,270-acre homestead farm of Stephen Vail, operator of the iron works in the early 1800s. It includes the Vail homestead and the cotton factory where his son Alfred, along with Morse, perfected the telegraph. The historic village, now a museum, also includes three houses moved from the center of Morristown when threatened with demolition by the right of way for Route 287 and the Morristown Urban Renewal Project.

It was at the Speedwell Iron Works in 1818 that the 90-horsepower engine of the *Savannah*, the first steamship to cross the Atlantic Ocean, was built. It was completed within a year at a cost of $4,000, and in 1819, the little vessel sailed from New York to Savannah, Georgia and thence to Europe, returning to America with "not a single bolt loose" according to her captain.

At the Speedwell Iron Works were manufactured important parts of the first American locomotives and the first cast iron plow used in America. A copy of Leonardo de Vinci's "Last Supper" cast in iron was also made at the iron works about 1840.

Among articles handled by the iron works under the direction of S. Vail and Son, proprietors, were "presses, cannon, comb, dry dock, jack, fulling mill, and book binders screws. Also heavy wrought iron work, bolts, connecting and piston rods, center and water wheel shafts, axles for railroad cars, pumps, all kinds of castings and valves for engines." A great deal of this work was done for the southern and South American trade.

Speedwell, before Vail took over, was the second slitting mill in Morris County. It was built about 1777 by Jacob Arnold and John Kinney of Morristown, but despite Kinney's experience in the iron business, it failed. In 1796, Arnold sold his interest to Dr. Timothy Johnes, minister of Morristown's First Presbyterian Church. Eighteen years later, Kinney's interest was sold to James C. Canfield who deeded it to Vail, including the trip hammer works, blacksmith shop, coal house, and turning shop.

The iron works consumed great quantities of coal to turn the raw iron ore into finished products. Typical was the year 1813 when the iron works used 200 tons of anthracite coal and 2 tons of bituminous coal to produce 100 tons of Scotch pig iron, 100 tons of American pig iron, 95 tons of wrought iron, 1,400 pounds of cast steel, and 1,000 pounds of brass and copper.

When Vail took over the 47-acre property in 1807, he first turned the barn in which the telegraph was perfected into a nail factory, then in 1829 converted it for cotton weaving.

The following advertisement, signed by Stephen Vail, appeared in the *Genius of Liberty* on January 30, 1810:

> S. Vail & Co. have for sale at Speedwell Iron Works near Morristown, sleigh-shoes laid with steel and chopping axes of first quality. Also iron screws and boxes for grist, fulling and paper mills and for book binding, tobacco printers, etc. Persons who wish any of the above articles made to any particular pattern will do well to apply as above, as they can be accommodated at short notice, and upon reasonable terms.

Faced with increasing competition from iron firms closer to the metropolitan market, the iron works was moved in 1873 to Brooklyn and the property was acquired by the Lidgerwood family. Until the death of John Lidgerwood in 1955, the historic barn where the telegraph was perfected was well maintained, but after its sale to a real estate firm, it was allowed to deteriorate.

The historic stone arch bridge separating the iron works and Speedwell Lake was built in 1891 after a heavy freshet swept away the dam, and the foundations of the old bridge were seriously undermined and its upper part swept away. The flood drained the water from the lake, which in 1838 had three islands: Grand Island, the largest; Isola Belle; and one composed of a few bogs.

The size of the original lake can be gleaned from the fact that a small side-wheeler type steamboat operated on it before 1900, for a number of years taking excursions around the lake.

The bridge, which carries Route 202 between Morristown and Morris Plains over the Whippany River, was rebuilt and the dam reconstructed in 1937 by the WPA, allowing the water to back up and refill the lake.

Speedwell Village, organized in 1966 as a non-profit, educational, and historical corporation, its operations hindered by lack of funds, was taken over by Morris County in 2002. The Park Commission assumed stewardship. The former Board of Trustees became the Friends of Historic Speedwell.

It was a big day in Morristown when the two houses were moved from the hollow 2 miles to Historic Speedwell. Preceded by a small army of tree trimmers, state highway department crews, utility men, and police, the houses were hauled up the steep grade of Spring Street hill, then towed down Speedwell Avenue to Speedwell Village. More than 3,000 bystanders watched in silence as the 230-ton Heslin house and the smaller Satchelle house were towed in the major east-west artery by 16-ton trucks to their new location. Each house rested on giant yellow I-beams and dollies with 8 and 12 airplane-size wheels.

The two houses are the last of five on the map General Washington drew of Morristown. The Satchelle house, built in 1771, was at 91 Spring Street, in the path of the town's urban renewal project. The Heslin house, built *c.* 1750, was

*WPA work crews reconstructed the Speedwell Lake dam, washed out in a heavy rainstorm, draining the lake and destroying the bridge that carried Speedwell Avenue over the Whippany River.*

in the right of way of Route 287. It was purchased for $25 at auction for the Morristown Historical Society. During the winter encampment of Washington's army in 1779 and 1780, it was used as an office by his officers.

Because of the Vail family's pioneering role in industry, transportation, and communication, Historic Speedwell Village is more than a typical economic unit of the early nineteenth century. It illustrates the origin of the American idea of progress that, during the course of the century, became an active value.

The Vail factory houses a number of working displays tracing the history of the telegraph from the beginning of electricity and electromagnetism to the modern computer. Some are on permanent loan from the Smithsonian Institution and others have been contributed by Western Electric Telegraph Company.

The Vail house was completely renovated by Stephen Vail in the 1840s. On-going restoration has revealed a central heating system he installed, plaster cornices, grained woodwork, and painted floors. Portraits of Stephen and his wife Bethiah, painted by Morse in 1837, hang in the main hall. The front door overlooks a greensward that was the garden in Vail's day.

In the wheel house, water powers a 24-foot over-shot wheel. By a system of gears, belts, and pulleys, the turning wheel drove a gristmill, a heavy grinder which made bone meal for fertilizer, and machinery in the adjoining factory. In

Vail's day, the water to power the wheel flowed underground from a high pond, filling a standpipe behind the building by gravity.

The huge water wheel, considered to be the largest in the state, was discovered on its side in the mud beside the building. It was restored to working order and now revolves with great speed.

The Ford cottage was probably built in the early 1800s by Gabriel Ford Jr., grandson of Colonel Jacob Ford whose home was General Washington's headquarters in the winter of 1779–1780. Moved from Morristown to an old foundation at the village, it retains its small paned windows and wide, untapered clapboards.

The L'Homedieu house is named after the pre-Revolutionary owner of its original site in Morristown. Although a dwelling of this size stood on the lot from 1777 to 1812, the present house is believed to date from the late 1820s. Its gambrel roof and recessed doorway are noteworthy. The building houses the gift shop and in the basement is a recreated Colonial kitchen.

A Revolutionary War veteran built the Moses Estey house in Morristown shortly after fire destroyed his first home in 1786.

The granary was built by the Vails on stone piers with spaces under its clapboards for ventilation. Handcrafted wooden farm tools and nineteenth-century ice harvesting equipment are on exhibit.

The 1849 carriage house once used to shelter the overflow of vehicles for the Vail family now contains a number of exhibits, including recreational and transportation vehicles and a display of butter making equipment.

On the main floor of the carriage house is a collection of original wooden patterns. The iron works cast iron in sand molds formed by using these

*This mansion was Stephen Vail's, owner of the Speedwell Iron Works. It contains portraits of Stephen and his wife Bethiah painted by Samuel F.B. Morse in 1837.*

wooden patterns. The technique was used to make gears, waterwheels, and parts for locomotives.

## LAFAYETTE RETURNS

In 1825, Lafayette, the French hero of the American Revolution, returned to Morristown 45 years after he brought General Washington the news in 1780 that a huge French fleet and soldiers were en route to aid the American colonies.

Early in the afternoon of July 14, a booming cannon informed the throngs of citizens on The Green that he had reached Whippany, and an hour later, a second salute told the expectant crowd that he was approaching Morristown escorted by officials and a military escort of the Morris Calvary.

He was conducted directly to The Green where a large reception platform and an arch had been erected. Here an address of welcome was delivered by Dr. Lewis Condict, to which Lafayette replied briefly. Later, he was escorted to a banquet at the Sansay house on DeHart Street attended by the county's most distinguished and wealthy men, ladies not being admitted. Later that evening, he attended another reception to meet the ladies of the town.

## THE RAILROAD ARRIVES

There was great excitement in Morristown in 1838 when the tracks of the fledgling Morris & Essex Railroad were laid across the Field Club grounds and through fields in front of Macculloch Hall to the terminus at Market Street. After leaving Convent, the original right of way curved west just east of Sneden's Crossing (now Normandy Parkway), crossed the Morris Turnpike (Route 24), and paralleled it to the Field Club grounds over what in the Gilded Age was to become the front lawns of millionaire's estates.

Construction of the railroad had been on men's minds since November 19, 1836 when the first meeting to consider it was held in Morristown. Some trouble was experienced with property owners in Convent and Morristown over whose property the railroad was to extend. They initially sought high fees for the privilege, an action that caused uncertainty as to just where and how the railroad would reach its Morristown terminus.

Extension of the railroad to Morristown made it possible for residents to get to Newark, Hoboken, and New York "in no time." It also provided a means of transportation for material goods for Morristown stores, which previously had relied on horse and wagon, and later for coal from the Pennsylvania coal fields to heat the houses and mansions.

One commuter always waited until the last minute to catch the train. He was James K. Colles. When the engine bell signaled the pending departure of the daily train, his family and servants in Macculloch Hall rushed out on the veranda or peered from the upper windows, not so much to see the wood-burning engine puff by as to see if he would catch the train.

It was his custom to remain at the breakfast table until the bell sounded. He would then hastily don his stovepipe hat and a dust coat and run across the field waving his napkin at the engineer. The train generally stopped for him. But if he missed it, he could be seen riding his horse frantically down the road to overtake it at the next stop.

The tracks of the railroad ran down the center of Railroad Avenue to a tiny wooden station at Maple and DeHart Streets. A siding branched off from the main track into a lumber yard at the site of the old Maple Avenue School (Now a double deck parking lot).

To circumvent the steep grade of Fort Nonsense hill in its westward march to Dover, railroad officials abandoned the Railroad Avenue route in 1848 and located the tracks on flat ground near the Whippany River. The Railroad Avenue tracks were ripped up and the avenue renamed Maple Avenue.

When the decision was made to move the railroad to flat ground, the two-room frame station at DeHart Street and Maple Avenue was moved to the rear of the property at 11 Maple Avenue where it was used for years as a shed. It was razed in 1959 after falling into disrepair. What happened to its bell, which was rung when the train was about to depart, remains a mystery.

In the beginning, the service was all passenger. Freight service started in 1839. The freight was carried on a flat car without sides or stakes, and covered by canvas. The conductor carried the way bills in his hat.

Morristown's second railroad station, a rambling frame Victorian building at Elm and Morris Streets, served passengers until 1870 when it was replaced with a red brick structure, two years after double tracks were completed from Hoboken to Morristown. The wooden freight house was opposite the passenger station with three tracks between the two buildings. One was the main track, the second a siding on which passenger cars were stored, and the third an unloading track for freight.

Behind the freight house was another unloading track and a spur serving the Day & Muchmore lumber yard and the Martin & Caskey coal yard and trestle, and a branch line to the Farm Service Exchange and American Feed Company. Further west was the rag house used for Whippany Paper Board Company stock. Near the present express building was the turntable and roundhouse. On the passenger station side was a water tank perched on a high bank, and beyond it a coal shed and bunk house where Italian men working on the gravel train lived.

The sidings all converged before the river was reached where a single track led over a timber trestle. Water Street, a grade crossing where you went up and then down again to cross the tracks, was where ashes were dumped onto the main track, then thrown over the bank daily by trackmen.

Almost hidden from view behind the new Delaware, Lackawanna & Western Railroad Station was the tiny station of the Morristown & Erie Railroad, which dates to 1895 when a charter was granted to the Whippany River Railroad to construct a 4-mile line from Morristown east to the paper mills at Whippany. The Whippany River Railroad formed a second company, the short-lived Whippany & Passaic River Railroad, in 1903 to extend a line to a connection with the Erie Railroad at Essex Fells. Later that year, the lines merged to form the Morristown & Erie Railroad, which prospered for nearly three quarters of a century until 1977 when it went into bankruptcy. Reorganized in 1982, it expanded with the lease of the Chester branch of the Dover & Rockaway Railroad and a small portion of the former Central Railroad of New Jersey High Bridge branch.

## THE MORRIS CANAL

In 1822, seven years before the railroad reached Morristown, the Morris Canal was conceived by George F. Macculloch, a Morristown millionaire, while fishing at Lake Hopatcong. While waiting for a fish to bite, he noticed that the waters of Lake Hopatcong flowed both east and west. Here, he thought, was water to fill a canal. "Why not," he asked himself, "a waterway across New Jersey connecting the Delaware and Hudson Rivers."

His enthusiasm overcame the questions of bankers and engineers whom he consulted. A fruitless attempt was made in 1824 to raise funds from the state. The backers of the enterprise, however, did obtain from the legislature a charter permitting the building of the canal with private funds. Hence, the Morris Canal and Banking Company was formed. Macculloch, after interesting New York investors in the canal, pulled out of the company, which with huge profits to all, did construct the canal, an accomplishment as significant to Morristown as its pioneering and Revolutionary War periods. It not only staggered skeptics, but astonished the imagination of all.

A preliminary survey disclosed that to cover the 55 miles between the two rivers, a canal 100 miles long would be required. The problem of hoisting canal

*The second Morristown railroad station, a frame structure on Morris Street, shows the Millionaires Express about to depart for New York c. 1924. The building on the right is the freight station.*

49

*These are the railroad marshalling yards at the foot of Elm Street. The building in the center is the station for the Morristown & Erie Railroad, which ran to Essex Fells.*

barges and lowering them again baffled engineers. In those days, locks were the customary method of changing levels in canals, but in the case of the Morris Canal almost 300 locks would have been required had not someone thought of a series of inclined planes and portages.

The first shovelful of earth was lifted on October 15, 1825, six years before the entire course of the canal from Phillipsburg on the Delaware River to Jersey City on the Hudson River was opened to commercial traffic. Then mules were used to pull barges loaded with coal from the Pennsylvania coal fields to heat Morristown homes and also goods to stock the shelves of Morristown stores.

The Morris & Essex Railroad, together with the Delaware & Raritan Canal, sounded the death knell of the Morris Canal at the dawn of the twentieth century. A committee that called itself the Morris Canal Parkway Committee was organized in an unsuccessful effort to perpetuate the waterway as a scenic attraction. In 1924, the state legislature, which had chartered the canal 100 years earlier, sealed its fate. Only small sections of the canal and a canal museum at Lake Hopatcong remain today.

## TOLL ROADS APPEAR

Earlier on March 9, 1801, the Morris Turnpike, New Jersey's first toll road, was constructed from Elizabethtown to Morristown. These roads were regarded as essential shortly after 1800. Better roads meant cheaper goods for the consumer, and easier accessibility to schools and churches.

Three turnpikes fanned out from Morristown to the west, but only one, the Morris Turnpike, from the east. The latter was built and financed in three sections, the first from Elizabethtown to Morristown, the second from Morristown to Stanhope, and the third to Newton. Most are now state highways.

Construction of the Morristown section proceeded slowly, but by 1810, it was paying dividends of 4.4 percent. Its route through Morristown was Washington Avenue, Morris Street, Spring Street, Speedwell Avenue, and Sussex Avenue.

The Union Turnpike, construction of which was started with $7,500 raised by a lottery, was chartered by the state legislature in 1804. Its route through Morristown was Speedwell Avenue above Sussex Avenue and Mountain Way in Morris Plains. The Washington Turnpike, now Route 24, began one-half mile west of The Green and ran through Mendham, Chester, and Schooley's Mountain.

In 1854, its toll rates were: wagon or carriage and one beast, 2¢; additional beast, 1¢; horse and rider or led horse or mule, 2¢; 12 calves, sheep, or hogs, 2¢; and 12 horses, mules, or cattle, 5¢.

Citizens seeking ways to save money by bypassing toll gates reverted to sabotage, crashing, or bypassing them. Typical was Mendham Road in Morris Township, which cuts through the woods around the toll house rejoining the toll road at the foot of Delbarton Hill. In 1854, a law was enacted imposing a penalty of not more than three years in jail or a $500 fine for breaking or destroying toll gates.

## DUSTY STREETS

Prior to the turn of the century, Morristown streets, dusty in the summer months, were sprinkled with water to keep the dust down. The crews performing this service collected fees from occupants of buildings on streets sprinkled. They purchased the water from the Morris Aqueduct Company and loaded it into wagons from hydrants. Toward the end of the sprinkling era, Dustoline, an oil-based liquid, was invented and used in place of water.

Some Morristown streets had a coating of gravel from a gravel pit on Harter Road purchased by the town. It made a fairly smooth surface in the winter and spring, but mushy mud in the summer and fall. The necessity for harder material for the busier streets was felt, resulting in prisoners in the county workhouse crushing stone for street surfaces. The stone was gathered from the fields and brought to the jail yard behind the courthouse.

## A THEATER TOWN AND THE LIBRARY LYCEUM

Morristown was a theater town. People came from miles around to attend performances at the Lyceum Theater (on South Street opposite Community Place). Favorites were the musicals and minstrel shows, featuring such greats as Edwin Booth, Joseph Jefferson, Lillian Russell, Lillie Langtry, and Fritz Kreisler.

Billboards with flaming lithographs told of the minstrel shows coming. It was always a big day in Morristown when the minstrel boys arrived, sometimes in their private cars on the Delaware, Lackawanna & Western Railroad. At noon, there was always a street parade. Stores closed to allow clerks to see the parade, while the Maple Avenue School was dismissed five minutes earlier to permit students to watch the minstrel performers and their band, usually 50 or 60 pieces in number, circle The Green and march down South Street to Lyceum Hall.

Started in 1875, the Lyceum became Morristown's cultural center. It housed the Morris Academy and the Morristown Library until the Washington Birthday fire in 1914, which gutted the three-story granite structure. Besides regular stage shows, the hall was used also for the monthly meetings of the Friday Evening Club. It was this group that brought the famous singers, authors, and lecturers to its meetings, which were attended for the most part by men and women in full evening dress.

In 1904, ten years before the fire which destroyed the building, a warning was issued that the structure was not safe. The directors of the library and Lyceum responded by installing some metal fire doors and voting that the Friday Evening Club could continue to occupy the hall at its own risk. The warning the club issued, however, sounded the death knell of the hall, which for years had been the principal gathering place in Morristown both for local residents and the opulent society flings of "the 400"—the people who constituted Morristown society.

The warning also served to inform residents, many of whom were unaware of its existence, that on the third floor above the gallery was a large room designed for dances. It was seldom used. There was also a removable sectional floor, which, when placed over the seats on the main floor, created a large area for social events best remembered by a $75,000 ball given by Richard A. McCurdy, president of the Mutual Life Insurance Company.

The entire interior was painted yellow. There was a semicircular gallery with terraced seats and four boxes, two on the main floor and two on the gallery floor.

Built before the days of fireproof construction at a cost of $65,000, the Library Lyceum opened in 1878. Basically, it was a structure of yellow pine built inside four walls of granite boulders from Jockey Hollow donated by the Morris Aqueduct Company.

The fire that destroyed the building consumed its library of 50,000 books, invaluable newspaper files, and portraits of two of Morristown's foremost citizens, Joseph Blatchey and William L. King. The fire, discovered at 5:30 a.m. by a watchman at a nearby stable who noticed smoke issuing from the building, burned out of control until 10:30 a.m. despite three powerful streams of water poured into the structure by firefighters.

Newspaper accounts reported the flames started in the basement near the hot air furnaces, themselves relics from the old Presbyterian Church that had burned, then made their way up through the floor and spread throughout the building, creating dense smoke, which made it impossible for firemen to enter the structure.

Two hours after the fire's discovery, it had eaten its way through the beams that supported the slate roof, causing it to cave in, sending flames and embers shooting high in the air. Some flaming brands fell on the roof of the boarding house across South Street, setting it afire.

*The Library Lyceum on South Street opened in 1878 and was Morristown's cultural center at the turn of the century. It was destroyed by fire, which consumed the library of 50,000 books, in 1914.*

## THE MAN WHO DREW SANTA CLAUS

Typical of the personages who appeared on the Lyceum's stage was Thomas Nast, the man who drew Santa Claus, who appeared with Walter Pelham, a Morristown resident, in 1885. Nast, billed as the greatest cartoonist of his time, gave exhibitions of rudimentary drawing, progressive drawing, and artistic work while Pelham did impersonations. On display in the hall were many of Nast's paintings and panels of his Caricaturama, each 9 feet by 12 feet in size.

Few of the original 33 Caricaturama panels exist today. The story is told that a painter, finding them in a garage, used them for drop cloths. One is on display in the Morristown–Morris Township Library. Another is owned by the Macculloch Hall Museum. A few others are in private collections. Combined, they illustrate the history of the United States from the landing of the Pilgrims at Plymouth Rock to the mid-1800s.

The one on display in the Morristown–Morris Township Library is part of Nast's crusade against the unpopular President Andrew Johnson. It shows Johnson on a merry-go-round, accompanied by General Grant, Secretaries Seward, Wells, and Randall, and Admiral Farragut. They arrive nowhere on their carousel. Their circular journey is decorated with many American flags upside down, a recognized international distress signal. Each flag bears the large number 37 (the number of states then in the Union), showing that all 37 states were in trouble.

Many of the 8,000 drawings Nast did—the majority in his Morristown studio—are in the possession of the Morristown–Morris Township Library, including the one panel of his Caricaturama.

For years, funds to preserve the original drawings in the library collection did not exist. Now, thanks to the foresight of Miss Caroline Foster, herself a woman of wealth, funds have been made available to preserve these drawings and sporting pictures. They include not only the rough pencil sketches made by Nast before penning the final illustration, but unpublished drawings of Santa Claus, political drawings, and sporting pictures.

Nast is one of three artists who may assume credit for establishing Morristown as a core of the Golden Age of Illustration (1870–1890). The others were Arthur Burdett Frost of Convent Station, whose hunting scenes have become collectors' items, and Homer Calvin Davenport of Morris Plains, a caricaturist made famous by William Randolph Hearst at the turn of the century. Clustered around them were numerous other literary and artistic personalities.

Prior to World War II, the names of Nast, Frost, and Davenport were relatively unknown in Morristown, despite the years they made the town their home. Then in the 1950s and 1960s, the Nast residence on Macculloch Avenue was

*Villa Fontana, a neo-classical Victorian mansion at Miller Road and Macculloch Avenue (c. 1900) was home of Thomas Nast, famed political cartoonist, from 1872 to 1902. Its appearance changed over the years. Now, it is a National Historical Landmark.*

registered as a National and State Historic Landmark and Frost prints, especially his famed hunting series, zoomed in demand, bringing higher and higher prices. Macculloch Hall Museum, a stone's throw from the Nast home, created a Nast display; the Town of Morristown replaced Santa Land with a Thomas Nast Village on The Green each Yule season; the post office issued a commemorative stamp honoring Nast; and Morristown sponsored a Thomas Nast Day.

In many of Nast's Christmas drawings, which appeared annually on the cover of *Harper's Magazine*, bits of old Morristown are easily identified. The drawing "Christmas Greens," which shows a boy and girl, their arms laden with Yuletime greens, has a fence and gate in the background similar to the unusual redwood fence that surrounded Nast's home. Another shows Santa Claus seated at a large desk, obviously Nast's own. Others show the steeples of the Church of the Assumption and the Second Presbyterian Church, rooftops, and the fireplace in Nast's home. Several of the Christmas drawings are actual portrayals of Nast and members of his family.

A national figure hailed by President Abraham Lincoln as "the best recruiting sergeant the Union ever had," Nast went on to further and greater fame as a political cartoonist whose Tammany Tiger, Republican Elephant, John Bull, Columbia, and Democratic Donkey became classics as national and international symbols.

While residing in Morristown, he rejected a bribe of $500,000 in gold to halt his biting political cartoons aimed at the "Boss Tweed Ring" and Tammany Hall corruption that was milking New York City of millions of dollars, which he is credited with destroying through his cartoons. The coming-out party he threw for his daughter Julia was attended by 600 of the nation's leaders, men of wealth, and artists, many of whom came to Morristown on special trains.

Nast lent his artistic efforts towards raising funds for charitable events. Included was the town-wide effort by prominent men and women in 1875 to raise funds to preserve Washington's headquarters purchased at auction two years earlier. Nast had much to do with the success of this venture, which raised almost $1,200 in one afternoon and evening. He worked early and late at the decorations and filled one of the largest rooms at the headquarters with his immense and humorous cartoons of scenes of the Revolution and the stories of George Washington.

One of the sketches represented "Washington Crossing the Delaware" astride an ice car on which was lettered "Delaware Ice Co." A year later, in 1896, he lent original sketches for the benefit of the Memorial Hospital annex.

The work and life of Arthur Burdett Frost is laid against a nostalgic pageant of Morristown's millionaires, many of whom he used as models in his paintings for which he drew upon the Morris County countryside, particularly the woodlands and fields around Morristown, the Troy Meadows, and the marshes of the Whippany River.

With many of the millionaires, including Charles Scribner, W. Alston Flagg, Marmaduke Tilden, William W. Shippen, Hamilton McKown Twombly, Ransom

H. Thomas, George Frelinghuysen, Robert Dumont Foote, Alexander H. Tiers, William R. Sheldon, Louis A. Thebaud, and Edward Randolph, he hunted grouse and woodcock, often pausing as they crossed fields to sketch one of the men of wealth in a sporting scene.

Because of his friendship and association with these men, it was not unusual or strange when his initial portfolio of hunting pictures was published in 1895 by Charles Scribner, whose estate "The Gables" on Van Buren Road overlooked Frost's pillared mansion "Moneysunk" on Treadwell Avenue.

This portfolio, only 2,500 copies of which were published, immediately established Frost's reputation as one of the finest American sporting artists of his time. His total output of paintings, a majority of them produced in the small studio at Moneysunk, has been estimated at 10,000. Included were illustrations for more than 90 books written by such famous authors as Theodore Roosevelt, Richard Harding Davis, Mark Twain, Frank Stockton, Joel Chandler Harris, Charles Dickens, and William Thackeray.

Many of Frost's paintings and sketches depict life in Morristown during the Gilded Age. They range from his drawing of the Morristown Gun Club, established by many millionaires on the estate of Henry Mellon in South Street, to Robert D. Foote, owner of one of the first automobiles in Morristown, striking a farmer's cart in South Street.

In 1895, Frost, who was color blind, took up the relatively new sport of golf. He resolved to break 100 and spent much of his spare time playing at the Morris County Golf Club, often pausing to sketch one of the millionaires, many of whom he used as models. Proof that he did break 100 on the golf course was the silver cup that he won in a club tournament in 1897.

Many of Frost's original paintings found their way into the homes of the millionaires, townspeople, and area clubs. Typical was Hamilton McKown Twombly, a close associate of Frost and a hunting companion, who had 29 illustrations of varied subjects. Another was the Morris County Golf Club, which has his paintings on display in the main lobby, and the exclusive Morristown Club, which besides his lithographs of hunting scenes has several originals of the Uncle Remus series.

Apart from Frost, Nast was followed on the stage of the Lyceum several months later by Homer Calvin Davenport of Morris Plains, the cartoonist William Randolph Hearst ordered to New York to draw political cartoons the day he purchased the *New York Journal* in 1903. Like Nast, he was a popular figure in society circles in Morristown and New York.

On one hand, Davenport was one of the elite group of millionaires; on the other, he was not. His bank account came nowhere near that of the people of wealth, his estate was not as lavish, his number of servants smaller, and his carriages fewer.

Yet, he rode to New York from Morris Plains each weekday at 8:15 a.m. on the "Millionaires Special," played poker with them during the trip, and like them was met at the railroad depot by a coachman driving a carriage. Noted for his biting political cartoons, he was a large importer and breeder of pure Arabian horses. He had the finest and largest private collection of pheasants and wild water fowl in America, and a pair of purebred Arabian stallions named Yaquis and Yama to pull his carriage.

Actors, writers, heavyweight boxing champions, politicians, artists, millionaires, and presidents visited "Red Gables," his home on the Mt. Tabor Road. Each guest left his penciled autograph on the wall of the spacious open porch. There were names like Bob Fitzsimmons, "Buffalo Bill" Cody, Thomas A. Edison, James Lawrence, William Jennings Bryan, Lillian Russell, Annie Russell, and scores of others.

Like Nast, Davenport was one of the highest paid cartoonists in America. Perhaps his most famous caricature was of Mark Hanna wearing a checkered suit with dollar signs. Hanna, who practically owned the United States then, wrote Davenport a letter requesting the dollar signs be omitted. That declined, he came to Morris Plains and was with Davenport until midnight, offering all sorts of favors if he would drop the dollar signs. But the artist still declined.

The barbecues at Davenport's estate, usually limited to 100 guests, were renowned. To them came the famous and the near-famous from two continents: artists, actors, boxing champions, political figures, show girls, and many of Morristown's millionaires. A buckboard would be sent to the Morris Plains Railroad Station on Saturday afternoon to pick up the crowds of show girls and

*The painting of turn-of-the-century golfers at the Morris County Golf Club was sketched by Arthur B. Frost, a noted artist and club member whose score was usually in the mid-80s. Most of the men are millionaires used as models by Frost.*

*After running out of money to restore the Lyceum as a modern playhouse, two millionaires, Grinnell Willis and Samuel H. Gillespie, bought it for $18,000, converting it into an armory.*

their escorts coming for the weekend parties, the largest of which was held in 1905 when Davenport left for the Lewis and Clark Exposition in Portland, Oregon.

## THE ARMORY

After the fire that destroyed the Lyceum, considerable money was spent remodeling the interior of the burned structure to provide a modern playhouse. When work stopped because of the expense, Grinnell Willis and Samuel Gillespie, two millionaire philanthropists, bought the building for $18,000 and converted it into an armory. The 300-member Morristown Infantry Battalion occupied the building for the first time in 1917. Newspaper accounts report $60,000 was spent equipping the battalion with Lee Enfield rifles and three machine guns, which were mounted on Ford cars.

The armory passed to the state in 1920 by deed from Willis for $45,000. The battalion was disbanded after the armistice. The armory gained fame in 1926 when many of the evacuees from the explosion at Picatinny Arsenal and Lake Denmark Naval Ammunition Depot were brought to it. When its capacity was reached, others were taken to the United States Hotel on The Green.

## HOSPITALS

The greater Morristown area had no hospitals until the dusk of the 1800s when, within two years of each other, Morristown Memorial Hospital and All Soul's

Hospital opened their doors, the former in the parsonage of the First Presbyterian Church purchased for $25,000, the latter in a former tavern that had been moved from Park Place to Mt. Kemble Avenue.

Greystone Park, a psychiatric hospital for the mentally ill, opened 23 years earlier on August 17, 1876 on a 450-acre tract in Hanover Township (now Morris Plains) as a much needed antidote for the overcrowded psychiatric asylum in Trenton where the initial patients came from.

First called the State Asylum for the Insane, its name was changed in 1924 to the New Jersey State Hospital at Greystone Park. But despite its size, airy patient wards, lush grounds, and self sufficient campus, it had no maternity ward or facilities for operations or to treat patients with broken limbs or diseases.

Over the years, its size expanded to 1,273 acres. It was constructed almost entirely of stone, brick, slate, and iron to reduce the risk of fire. Its construction was financed by a $25-million appropriation passed by the state legislature.

Greystone, which served seven North Jersey counties, operated like a small city with its own 368 herd dairy, hog raising pens, tailor, farm, cattle, fire department, and sewerage and coal plants that helped light and heat the facility. A mass of tunnels beneath the hospital buildings ensured that patients and staff did not have to venture outside. The Greystone Annual Report for 1890 described the causes of insanity of most patients committed to the hospital as "old age, overwork, heat stroke, menopause and childbirth."

Major additions increased the size and patient capacity over the years. Included was the dormitory building for 600 patients opened in 1901; the clinic building for 100 patients in 1923; the reception building for 250 patients in 1927; the "Senile" building, later converted to a childrens' unit housing 27 patients, and the tuberculosis building with a capacity of 125 patients, both opened in 1931; and the 480-bed Abell building in 1957. Reconstruction of the original building with the addition of fourth-floor wards and the erection of outside dining halls and employees' quarters greatly increased capacity. Other buildings were extensively remodeled and extended. Included were four wings on the dormitory building and two additional housing units adjacent to the childrens' unit in 1949, providing a total of 900 beds.

By 1968, the number of patients had increased to 4,345 and the number of employees to 1,977. By the 1980s, inadequate staffing, an increasing number of complaints, lax security of patients, and buildings falling into disrepair, sometimes leaving patients without toilets or heat, became rampant because the state could not find enough carpenters, plumbers, and other tradespeople to fill the low-paying jobs.

In 1988, the hospital failed inspection and faced the loss of $5.1 million in federal funds. A year earlier, a Superior Court judge had ordered a reduction in the number of patients in the admissions ward after hearing testimony of "intolerable, oppressive and dangerous conditions." In 2000, Governor Christie Whitman ordered the hospital closed and a new hospital built within three years.

A historic building, the home of Reverend Timothy Johnes, the First Presbyterian Church minister when General George Washington was in Morristown, became the first Morristown Memorial Hospital when it accepted its first patients October 17, 1893. Located on the site of the Mid-Town Shopping Center, it served until 1898 when a three-story red brick building was erected to the rear of the parsonage, which was no longer able to meet the needs of an expanding population. With the abandonment of the Johnes house as a hospital building, it was purchased by Charles M. Drake and moved across Morris Street. It served as a tenement house for many years until it was partially burned, fell into disrepair, and was razed.

At the time, the hospital had 15 beds and a staff of 5 nurses, a student nurse, cook, laundress, and janitor plus its first debt, a $10,000 mortgage incurred in the purchase of the Johnes house.

The new hospital building was financed by George G. Kip, a millionaire New York lawyer, as a memorial to his wife. The original structure had 28 beds and six private rooms. The west wing of the hospital was built in 1905; the north wing, featuring a maternity ward, in 1914; the Havermeyer Contagious Unit, a gift of Peter H.B. Frelinghuysen, in 1917; the Helen Hartley School of Nursing in 1920; and the nurses' home in 1922.

In 1924, the hospital's last horse-drawn ambulance was replaced with a new motorized vehicle. By 1930, donations, bequests, and trusts enabled the hospital to purchase an electrocardiograph, enhancing the ability to diagnose and treat heart ailments.

Morristown Memorial Hospital was built on the vision and determination of many residents in Morristown who recognized the importance of having a premiere hospital. Equally important was the hospital's need to rely on philanthropic contributions and the dedication of an influential group of women who formed the Women's Association as early as 1893. By the 1950s, the need for a large scale enlargement of facilities became apparent. Realizing room did not exist at the Morris Street site for the type of hospital Morristown residents expected, the trustees authorized what some considered a drastic move to Madison Avenue where a new, enlarged, and modern hospital was erected.

The land on which the hospital stands was donated by C. Henry Mellon, a cousin of Andrew Mellon, and his sister Eleanor whose estate comprised the major portion of the 44 acres donated, plus the estates of Colonel and Mrs. Franklin D'Olier and Mrs. Ridley Watts, both millionaires.

The doors of the new hospital opened in 1953. Since then, expansion has gained momentum each year as the number of patients increased. In 1973, a $10-million Jefferson wing expansion was completed, doubling hospital space to more than 476,200 square feet and increasing parking facilities. In 1991, the hospital was designated as a level-two trauma center, one year before dedication of the Malcolm Forbes amphitheater, a surgical wing, and a three-story parking garage.

The construction was quickly followed by the erection of the Carol G. Simon Cancer Center with its own parking garage; a $40-million 256-unit apartment

*The first Memorial Hospital was once the home of Reverend Timothy Johnes, minister of the First Presbyterian Church. It was purchased from Mrs. Eugene Ayres in 1893 for the hospital.*

complex to replace Franklin Village apartments and provide housing for the hospital staff; and a children's wing.

To help renovate facilities and finance expansion programs, area industries and foundations contributed large sums of money. Typical was the Forbes Foundation, which contributed $500,000 in 1937, the Mennen Company, which gave $200,000, and the Beneficial Management Company, which gave $250,000, both in 1988.

While Morristown Memorial Hospital was renovating and expanding, All Soul's Hospital across town was facing tough sledding. The Sisters of Charity, who operated All Soul's, announced in early 1970 that the hospital had dropped to a point where it was no longer possible to run it in a "financially solvent manner." They set a date of February 28, 1970 for closing the hospital. The medical staff immediately went to court, the first step in an all-out effort to keep the financially stricken hospital open.

The announcement came after the trustees backed out of a deal by which the hospital would have shared the cost of new x-ray equipment, a report that the nursing school diploma program would be phased out, and the closing of the maternity ward. The Sisters of Charity, faced with a $2.5-million mortgage debt, confirmed that they had been talking merger with Morristown Memorial Hospital since late in 1969.

In July 1977, a management firm took over operation of the Community Medical Center, as All Soul's became known. A year later, in 1978, they filed for bankruptcy when unable to pay the $1.3 million owed creditors. In August, Morristown Memorial Hospital purchased its bankrupt crosstown neighbor and renamed it The Mount Kemble Division of Morristown Memorial Hospital. Since then, it has been devoted to long-term care, ambulatory, and rehabilitation services.

All Soul's Hospital had opened in 1892 in the former Arnold Tavern, which had been moved to Mt. Kemble Avenue (now the site of the hospital parking lot). The ballroom of the tavern was turned into a chapel and the dining room became the hospital ward. By 1893, the operating room was illuminated by gas, a horse-drawn ambulance had been secured, a steam laundry plant installed, and stables built for horses and cows. During the first year, 231 patients were admitted from all sections of Morris, Sussex, and Somerset Counties.

Three men, all millionaires, paid off the debt on the old building in 1901. They were Frederick Olcott, who the year before had equipped the operating room with the latest instruments; Anthony F. Brady; and Thomas F. Ryan.

In 1907, the Van Buren property, known as Mount St. Michael's Sanatorium, on the opposite side of Mt. Kemble Avenue, was acquired by the hospital. Seven years later, a fundraising campaign raised $100,000 to finance conversion of the sanatorium into a hospital. The cornerstone-laying ceremony for the new All Soul's Hospital was held May 20, 1917.

*The first All Soul's Hospital was the former Arnold Tavern. Though extended and enlarged, it retained many of the distinctive features that characterized it when it was General Washington's headquarters in 1777. It was destroyed by fire in 1918.*

There was one small private hospital at 36 Maple Avenue in Morristown. It was operated by Dr. Clifford Mills, who was prominent in the field of general surgery. It operated from 1918 to 1942.

## THE THREAT OF FIRE

Fire was a major concern, especially in the business district, before Morristown was incorporated in 1865 and the first fire department was organized two years later. From the days of the bucket brigade and hand-drawn hose carts, through the era of horse-drawn steamers and ladder trucks, fire associations existed, the first dating to July 26, 1797. But their equipment was meager, a hand-drawn engine purchased for $250 in 1836 and another the following year.

The Morristown Fire Association, incorporated in 1837, raised money by assessments levied on each of the buildings within the town limits. With this, they acquired equipment and built seven cisterns on the corners of important streets to supply water. The initial hook-and-ladder company was formed in 1859, but the organization was weak, the equipment of its truck consisting only of five ladders and two fire hooks.

In the 50 years from 1867 to 1926, there were 1,291 fires, with the fewest in any single year being in the first year and the most in 1910 when firemen answered 80 alarms. On several occasions, additional equipment was rushed to Morristown by train from points as distant as Newark.

Many treasures, valuable collections, and priceless works of art were lost in destructive fires that engulfed a number of the early Madison Avenue mansions, especially those constructed of wood in the days before the era of fireproof construction, modern firefighting equipment, and alarm systems.

Typical was the blaze on January 1, 1912 that completely destroyed "Cecilhurst," the three-story mansion of Adolph De Bary with its contents of costly rugs, tapestries, and art treasures. Other mansions were more fortunate, suffering only partial damage. Included was that of Mrs. George W. Jenkins (aunt of Marcellus Hartley Dodge) at 238 South Street, from which she was carried by firemen on October 20, 1930; the residence of Charles H. Mellon, one of the most impressive on Madison Avenue; and the Seth Thomas Jr., George T. Cobb, and John D. Canfield mansions.

Many reasons were given for the large number of destructive fires. Blame for the blaze that leveled the Phillip Livingston residence on Madison Avenue on May 2, 1903 was attributed to a delay in sounding the alarm, a poor water supply, and ineffective hose. The Cobb fire was traced to a defective flue, others to inadequate furnaces, poor electrical wiring, overheated pipes, and leaking gas.

Cecilhurst, the George H. Danforth estate built in 1876, was rented, repaired, and improved by Hamilton McKown Twombly in 1890 as a residence while his new estate was under construction.

To sound the alarm in the business district, the Fire Department Committee in 1875 arranged with the First Presbyterian Church to have a rope attached to the church bell and secured in the outer hall of the church in a locked box to which each policeman had a key. In later years, the bell in the cupola of the county courthouse sounded the alarms.

The first motorized apparatus, a Simplex Auto Chemical Truck, was delivered to the department in 1909. It carried two 35-gallon tanks and two hand extinguishers. The initial motorized ladder truck was built for and operated by the Resolute Hook and Ladder Company in 1912, succeeding equipment pulled by Tom and Jerry, two horses.

One of the first big fires occurred in 1877 when the frame South Street Presbyterian Church was totally destroyed. Four years later, in 1881, two women lost their lives in a fatal fire which destroyed Miss Hunter's boarding house on South Street. In 1890, the Farrelly building was destroyed with a loss of $100,000.

In 1899, the ice house on the east shore of Mills Pond in Burnham Park and nearby barns were demolished by flames. One of the most destructive fires occurred in 1894 when five buildings in the rear of the McAlpin and Caskey properties on North Park Place were gutted. Later that year, the blacksmith shop and a portion of the machine shop at the Speedwell Iron Works were leveled.

The century ended with the destruction of what had been considered the "fireproof" Folly building and adjacent stores that housed a grocery, shoe shop, confectionery, and barber shop. On the second and third floors of the buildings several families were burned out of their apartments.

## THE YMCA

The year was 1874 and horses and buggies had it all their own way, circling The Green in traffic that traveled in both directions, not one way as today. On North Park Place, a new sign was tacked up over the entrance to a second floor walk-up room in a two-story frame building that housed the Morristown Post Office. It stated: "YMCA Rooms."

It was the result of work by several men who believed the "Y" would be a good influence on backsliders of the church. The first quarters were simple and sparse, just a large room with chairs that served for early meetings and prayer groups. After a few meetings, the idea of the YMCA caught on and the organization expanded its space to the entire second floor of the building, including a reading room and a parlor.

The organization date was January 2, 1874. The place was the Baptist Church on The Green where Dr. Frederick Wooster Owens and Reverend Thomas E. Souper called for a public meeting to discuss formation of a YMCA in Morristown. Earlier informal meetings had been held in the home of Dr. Owens on South Street.

By 1881, there was a movement for a new and complete association building. But things moved slowly until the formation of a Women's Auxiliary in 1883, which lost no time in starting a fundraising drive that netted $30,000 within a few years, a sufficient amount to construct a building on South Street near DeHart Street, which was dedicated October 10, 1889.

A brochure described the Y as "a pleasant resort for young men." It listed attractions, including bowling alleys, bathrooms supplied with both tubs and showers, hot and cold water, a dressing room with 95 lockers, gymnasium, reading room, and game room for checkers, dominoes, and chess.

With establishment of the new building, the Y began broadening its activities and, in 1890, formed a junior department for boys between the ages of 12 and 16. About the same time, a Y bulletin suggested a ladies gymnasium class be instituted. It wasn't until World War I, however, that the building was opened to women and girls on a "part-time basis."

From the 1890s to 1909, the YMCA moved forward at a steady pace, offering new programs, including a two week camping program, first at Barnegat Bay and later at Jefferson Pond and Allamuchy Lake near Hackettstown.

Gradually the need for a new, larger, more modern building developed and, by 1911, a fundraising campaign seeking $100,000 was underway. Property was purchased on Washington Street at the intersection of Western Avenue for $14,000 and a building constructed for $98,000. In succeeding years, several additions were added to the structure.

## MOVIES COME TO MORRISTOWN

Movies came to Morristown in the dusk of the 1800s. First shown in the Lyceum Theater, they were a big hit. People came from miles around to view them. Other films were shown in 10¢ arcades. One was on Washington Street near High Street. A larger one was in the Banner Building. Another, started as a full scale amusement enterprise, was at 18 Park Place.

*This apparatus was an early horse-drawn hook-and-ladder vehicle used to fight fires in Morristown before organization of the fire department.*

*The Palace Theater in Speedwell Avenue, Morristown's first movie house, was built by Antonio Esposito in 1910. Its prominence was eclipsed when the Park Theater opened.*

It was the Palace Theater, however, that became the principal show house in Morristown in the late 1800s and early 1900s. Located on Speedwell Avenue, it could accommodate 100. It was eclipsed when the Park Theater was built on the site of the Park House. Several years later, the Jersey Theater opened on Washington Street.

Combined, the three theaters plus the 10¢ movie arcades gave Morristown the nickname of "Movie Town." Two attempts to add new theaters failed. After the Lyceum burned, considerable money was spent remodeling the interior of the structure to provide a modern playhouse, but the money ran out before the remodeling was completed.

Another early plan failed, but at the cost of thousands of dollars. Antonio Esposito unsuccessfully attempted to excavate the rock back of the Palace Theater to extend it to Prospect Street. The scheme provided for a grandiose theater using the foyer of the old Palace Theater for its entrance.

The flickering black and white movies were not the only attraction at the movie houses. Great actors and actresses, metropolitan opera stars, authors, lecturers, well known comedians, and minstrels appeared before the footlights, especially those on the stage of the Lyceum.

"Those were the days of bathing beauty contests, amateur nights and live elephants on the stage," Dominick Caravaggio recalled. He got his start at the

Palace Theater in the 1920s playing piano, accordion, and harp as part of the show's vaudeville act.

"I'll never forget the time Jackie Kennedy came into town to see a movie," Caravaggio noted. "Nobody knew she was there, not even the rest of the audience. I had some scoop. So I gave the *Daily Record* a call. They sent a photographer."

It was not until 1937, however, that Morristown's fourth theater, The Community on South Street, was built by the Walter Read organization. Admission then was 25¢ for a matinee and 75¢ for the Saturday evening show.

Described as a theater ahead of its time, its grand opening featured a buffet and reception for leading citizens of the town. The opening movie was *Nothing Sacred* with Carole Lombard and Frederic March.

All who attended were impressed with the simple beauty of the theater, finished in white and buff with dark blue carpeting and seats upholstered in dark red. Indirect lighting furnished illumination.

Construction employing 130 men was started after several hearings before the Board of Aldermen, marked by mass appearances of several hundred workmen who stormed the board room with signs demanding "we want work." The aldermen first refused to approve plans for a small theater, holding that a building on the site, adjoining the municipal building and across from Saint Peter's Episcopal Church and the Morristown–Morris Township Library, both noted for their architectural designs, should be in keeping with the dignity of its surroundings.

Unfortunately, it was a theater destined for hard times. By the 1970s, it changed hands, fell into disrepair, and finally closed by the end of the decade. Boarded up and in disrepair, it was a symbol of the decline of the Morristown business district through the recession of the early 1990s. The roof leaked, plumbing, heating, and air conditioning lived on borrowed time, and paint was peeling from the exterior columns.

The turning point was in 1994 and 1995 when The South Street Theater Company, a non-profit group, was formed. In 1999 and 2000, it scheduled 80 programs. Volunteers rolled up their sleeves and started a massive renovation project spurred by a $7.6-million capital building program. Money began to flow in. The Kirby Foundation donated $450,000; the Dodge Foundation, $100,000; and the former Warner Lambert Pharmaceutical Company, $500,000.

Today, The Community Theater has once again become a vibrant anchor of town life with nearly 100 events scheduled, thanks to the sweat and equity hundreds of volunteers invested in the ailing performance house, determined to make it into a center of culture in Morristown.

It is one of a few such facilities serving northwestern New Jersey with a variety of live stage entertainment, including ballet, drama, dance, choral groups, symphony orchestras, and popular artists.

The volunteers who achieved this said the first performance felt as if the clock had been turned back to the time when The Community was the theater to which audiences came from far and near. That night, a sense of excitement permeated the comfortable interior as the theater took on a semblance of its former grandeur.

One of the big movie hits at The Community was the showing of the world film premiere of one of the *This is America Series*. All of the film was shot in Morristown and dozens of local residents appeared in it, many in leading roles. Entitled *Who is Delinquent*, it included street scenes, scenes in the main courtroom of the courthouse, the Church of the Redeemer, and the city room of the *Daily Record*.

Today, Morristown has only two theaters, The Community and a 10-screen theater in Headquarters Plaza. When the Park Theater building was razed for Headquarters Plaza, the Park Theater packed its movie reels and popcorn and moved to the Jersey Theater, which had become the Morristown Triplex Theater.

The Park Theater, originally known as the Lyons Theater, was erected at a cost of $60,000 by James T. Lyons in 1915, five years after Antonino Esposito erected the Palace Theater. Harry Roth took over the Lyons Theater, then the Jersey Theater, selling out his interest in both theaters in 1938.

The Jersey Theater, called the Paramount Public Theater when it opened in 1924, was closed for 22 years before the Park Theater moved in, its bare marquee towering over the Washington Street sidewalk. The Triplex Theater, which replaced it, was razed in 2000 for an apartment complex.

## MORRISTOWN'S EARLY HOTELS

In the early nineteenth century, people loved to come to Morristown from the metropolitan cities for the salubrity of its climate, the unspoiled natural beauty of its countryside, and to stay at one of its hotels, most of which were clustered around the business district. Some came for just the summer months; others were year-round boarders. For some, it was the varied menus; for others horse and buggy rides in the countryside.

The hotels where they stayed have long since been razed and their locations rebuilt with stores and office buildings, but in their time, they prospered. Their death knell was the automobile, electrification of the Delaware, Lackawanna & Western Railroad, and bus lines to the metropolitan cities, all of which combined to make it economically unfeasible to operate a hotel.

Most of the hotels maintained elaborate stables, both for horses for hire and for the horses of people staying at the hotel. Some kept purebred racing stock, which could be seen racing every Saturday at the racetrack at the end of South Street.

A few of these stables still exist, their red brick buildings long since converted to other uses. On the sides of several, the faint outline of advertisements painted on the brick for products long since forgotten can be seen.

In the mid- to late-1800s and early 1900s, the hotels ranged from the United States Hotel, the New Jersey Hotel, and the Park House, all facing The Green; the Mansion House and the Avenue House on Washington Street; The Morristown Inn on South Street; the Farmers Hotel and Piper's Hotel, both on Market Street; and the West End Hotel on Speedwell Avenue. Some were sumptuous in their decor. Others were plain frame buildings, some with a lawn in front, others with just hitching posts for horses and carriages.

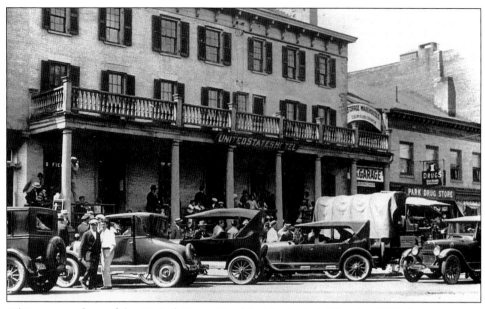

*This scene in front of the United States Hotel in North Park Place in 1926 shows evacuees from the Picatinny Arsenal Lake Denmark Naval Ammunition Depot explosion arriving and an army truck unloading mattresses.*

The numbers of persons coming to Morristown, celebrated for its healthfulness and as a place for invalids to recover, became so great that New York businessmen solicited William Gibbons, whose Madison estate became Drew University, to construct a boarding house and hotel with all modern improvements. First called the Morris County House, its name was afterwards changed to the New Jersey Hotel.

Construction started in the 1840s on West Park Place of what was perhaps the most luxurious hotel in Morristown through the Depression, despite its short life. The imposing structure extended back to Maple Avenue. Built at a cost of $200,000, it had towering white Doric columns three stories high guarding its entrance.

Built of brick and brownstone with a copper roof, the hotel, now the site of Epstein's Department Store, was likened by a New York newspaper to "A.T. Stewarts imposing uptown store in New York" and described as "the finest hotel in the country."

It opened in 1842 with a grand ball that attracted the cream of society from as far as New York. Two African-American footmen in knee breeches and crimson vests greeted guests at the elegant entrance. Inside, the floors were hushed by velvet carpets. The parlors were complete with carved and gilded furniture, most of it imported from Paris, and reflected on all sides by huge mirrors.

Four years after it opened, a fire in O'Hara's Tavern, the former Continental Army Storehouse next door, spread rapidly to the hotel, destroying it despite extra firefighting equipment rushed to Morristown by train from Newark. All the guests were saved except one, a Mr. Bailey, who was burned to death. After the fire, a fence was erected around the blackened ruins.

The Mansion House on Washington Street near Schuyler Place was perhaps the most popular hotel. Its meals were excellent and the rooms well ventilated. It was the headquarters for many of the professional men and women, particularly those of the stage. When some well known play in New York came to Morristown, usually for a one-night stand, the cast stayed at the Mansion House for the night, leaving for the city in the morning. It was also the stopping off place for lawyers and jurors during court terms.

The hotel maintained a large stable where some of the finest racing and trotting horses were kept, their owners and trainers living at the hotel. At that time, there was a racetrack at the lower end of South Street (now Seaton Hackney County Park) where some of the best trotting races took place on Saturday afternoons, complete with bookies soliciting bets.

During the winter months when there was sufficient snow on the ground, the hotel was the mecca for semi-weekly races with horse and sleigh between the hotel and the Mansion House in Madison. Besides the bookies soliciting bets, there were prizes for the winners.

Started in 1864, the original frame Mansion House was razed in 1878 and replaced with a three-story, 60-room structure with a red pressed brick front

*The Mansion House in Washington Street was bought by B.C. Guerin in 1864. He built new stables, sheds, and carriage houses, and rebuilt the frame hotel. In 1878, it was razed and an 80-room brick structure was erected.*

and a two-story piazza. Considered one of the finest commercial hotels in the Morristown area, it attracted many traveling men.

The large barns, livery stable, and sheds behind the Mansion House were destroyed by a fire on March 14, 1907 started by two men who afterwards were apprehended and sentenced to state prison on arson charges.

The United States Hotel, located on North Park Place where the Park Square Building stands today, had a long porch overlooking The Green, one of the hotel's chief attractions. It was termed "one of the most popular meeting spots of the nineteenth and early twentieth centuries" by many local residents and hotel guests who spent hours in the porch's rocking chairs sitting, chatting, and watching the crowds go by.

It was the Morristown terminus for stages bringing passengers from the Watnong Station, located near Lake and Lake Valley Roads, of the New Jersey & Pennsylvania Railroad, which went bankrupt before a connection could be made with the Delaware, Lackawanna & Western Railroad in Morristown. More popularly known as the "Rock-A-Bye-Baby" Railroad because of its rough road bed, its single track ran from Whitehouse through Mendham and Brookside to the Watnong Station.

Park House on East Park Place, one of three hotels on The Green, was a popular place for commuters. It also had a large porch which overlooked The Green and was a popular place to sit and watch the crowds go by. In 1875, it was turned halfway around on its foundation to become the Park Apartments. At this time, the rear frame portion was razed to make room for the Park Theater.

What was considered the most fashionable hotel or inn in Morristown was the Morristown Inn, a rambling three-story frame structure with porches overlooking South Street. Located on the site of the present Community Theater, it had a large clientele of year-round boarders.

Perhaps the most famous of the Inn's guests was Hettie Green, whom the newspapers tabbed "The Witch of Wall Street" and who was rated the wealthiest woman in the United States. She wanted her daughter Sylvia to be married in fashionable Saint Peter's Episcopal Church, located diagonally across South Street from the inn, to Matthew Astor Wilkes, great-grandson of the first John Jacob Astor.

The wedding occurred on February 23, 1909. The groom slipped into Morristown the night before the wedding. Mrs. Green and her daughter arrived the next morning in the chartered pullman car "Ivorydale" attached to the morning train.

After the wedding ceremony, Mrs. Green put on one of the most elaborate wedding breakfasts ever seen in Morristown. Although she was said to be eccentric and extremely close and sharp on the bargain, she bequeathed the church $1.2 million when she died in 1916.

As a child, she had spent her summers in Morristown, to whose well-to-do Howland family she was related. While she owned hotels and apartment houses in New York, she preferred the quiet and beautiful surroundings of the inn and the delightful atmosphere of Morristown.

71

Down Market Street was the Farmer's Hotel. It wasn't an imposing establishment, doing more of a bar business than renting of rooms. It did, however, accommodate many of the stock companies that came to Morristown playing a week's stand at the Lyceum Theater. Its owner Henry Hedden also maintained a stable where some of the blooded race horses were kept for the races at the South Street track. The three-story frame structure, located almost opposite Maple Avenue, was razed before World War I.

Further up Market Street on the opposite side of the street was Piper's Hotel, more of an eating establishment and drinking house than a hotel. It did, however, have a few rooms on the upper floors for transient customers. Its site is now part of the Epstein's Department Store property.

The Avenue House on the corner of Washington Street and Western Avenue (Former site of the Morristown YMCA) advertised "baths, gas in rooms, billiard tables, hot and cold water and good stabling for horses." The hotel, which had 60 rooms, opened in 1863 and was sold in 1886 to the St. Hilda School, which enclosed the property with a high board fence.

The Morris County Sportsmen Club rifle group was organized at a meeting in the hotel in 1875. For a practice range, they secured the grounds of the Luce Farm and built a rifle range where matches were held.

Other hotels included the West End Hotel with its large front lawn atop a knoll at the junction of Speedwell Avenue and Spring Street. It was later known as the City Hotel and the Morris and Sussex Hotel. It was razed in 1898 to provide a site for a three-story brick store and apartment building.

The men who stayed in these hotels were particular about their clothes. Morristown clothing stores in the early and mid-nineteenth century started carrying as fine a line of clothing as could be purchased in the metropolitan cities. Typical was an advertisement by C.H. Mulford and Son:

> Shirts of the most elegant style. Nothing but Wamsutta linen 200 fine being used. Perfect fitting. Sizes 13 to 17 1/2 inches Neck. Also wrist bands stitched so any lady can finish and have the pleasure and credit of making husband's or brother's shirts such as sell for $3. Our price is $1.25. Boys size $1.

Today, only four hotels directly serve Morristown, only one of which is in the business district. They include The Headquarters Plaza Hotel, a towering 10-story steel and glass structure on Speedwell Avenue; The Westin Hotel, the former Governor Morris Hotel, on Whippany Road; the Best Western Hotel on the site of a former mansion at 270 South Street; and the Madison Hotel at 1 Convent Road, Morris Township.

# 4. An Appetite for Learning

That the advantages of education were a necessity for the children of Morristown where a willingness for culture and education prevailed among the inhabitants can be gleaned from an old trustees book of the First Presbyterian Church, which recorded approval for a schoolhouse to be built on The Green on January 12, 1767. Small and crude, it was one of the first buildings erected on The Green, then a rough, unkempt piece of land partly covered with oak and walnut trees. There is no description of this first schoolhouse, its exact location, who the teacher was, the grades and subjects taught, or the number of pupils.

The first documented record of a school teacher was a brief undated statement in a local newspaper that "Andrew Wilson was a teacher in the Classical School," one of a score of private schools and academies that sprang up in Morristown in the first half of the nineteenth century, mostly in private residences.

There was keen rivalry between these schools. Many flourished for only a short period and had few students. At one point, there were 14 private schools on South Street and 9 on Maple Avenue. Only two started in the nineteenth century survive today, The Peck School and the Morristown School, now Morristown-Beard. The death knell of the others was sounded by the opening of Morristown's first public school on Maple Avenue in 1869.

It was not until after the mid-1880s that large boarding schools began to make an appearance. Several are of note, such as Miss Dana's Boarding and Day School for Young Ladies, described as a school ahead of its time, located on the site of the Chase Bank on South Street; the Morristown-Beard School on Whippany Road; and Delbarton School on the Mendham Road.

Miss Dana's school closed in 1913 following her death from cancer, the all-boys Morristown School became co-educational after merging with the Beard School founded in Orange in 1891, and the Delbarton School, operated by the Benedictine monks, like Morristown-Beard, abandoned its boarding school policy and became a day school.

Three of Morristown's major private schools are located in what once were the mansions of Morristown's millionaires of the Gilded Age. Delbarton, mansion of Luther Kountze, New York banker, was purchased for $155,000 in 1925 by the Benedictine monks, 14 years before the school opened. In 1947, the Peck School purchased Linderwold, the 10-acre estate of John Claflin, an associate of J.P. Morgan and one of the foremost dry good merchants in the world. In 1930, the Religious Teachers of St. Lucy Filippi purchased for $125,000 the estate of Samuel H. Gillespie and established the Villa Walsh Academy for girls.

The first Washington Valley School at the intersection of Washington Valley Road and School House Lane in Morris Township, unlike many early schoolhouses, while not a building of beauty, contained many facilities other schools lacked. A description of an early 1800s school in the *History of Morris County 1739 to 1882* stated:

> The school building was constructed of logs and instead of glass for windows sheep skins were stretched over the apertures. These windows had one virtue—they were an effectual screen to prevent pupils from being interrupted in their exercises by what was going on outside. The time was regulated by an hour glass, and pupils drank water from a tumbler made of a cow's horn or a ground shell. The common school was hardly considered a school in those days unless the wack of the ruler or the whistle of the whip was frequently heard.

The initial Washington Valley Schoolhouse was built in 1813 when the people in the valley decided their children needed an education. It was constructed by the labor of many parents. Others paid tuition, supplied the firewood, or did necessary repairs.

In 1869, the people of the valley decided the old schoolhouse was not large enough for the growing population. The new school, dominated by a white cupola, was built of red brick with white trim at a cost of $2,025. In the 1880s, the girls of the area raised money for the bell. The interior contained a cloakroom and a kitchen in addition to the single classroom. Inside there were wooden shutters on the windows. The room was illuminated by eight kerosene lamps.

Young men in Morristown through the 1800s usually attended the Morris Academy started November 5, 1782 with 33 students in a little building on South Street on the site later occupied by the Library Lyceum, which purchased the academy property (opposite Community Place) for $10,000 in stock with the understanding that six rooms would be reserved for the academy.

The academy placed its educational stamp on Morristown for 125 years. It was originally conceived by 24 men, each of whom subscribed £25 for one share of stock. The lot for the academy was purchased the following year for £30 from the Trustees of the First Presbyterian Church.

In 1891, the academy offered classes in Latin, Greek, French, German, mathematics, physics, and chemistry. Tuition charges at the time of opening were: mathematics and surveying, 50 shillings per quarter; English studies, 12, 15, and 16 shillings per quarter, and French, 30 to 40 shillings per quarter.

One of the great annual events in Morristown at the dawn of the nineteenth century was the annual play or "exhibition" presented by the boys of the academy.

With the money earned from admission charges, averaging $210 annually, the academy building was kept in repair and a bell purchased for its cupola.

In an 1809 copy of the *Palladium of Liberty*, an early newspaper, this advertisement appeared:

> Drastic exhibition on Thursday and Monday evenings the 5th and 9th of October next, will be presented by the students of the Morris Academy Cumberland's Celebrated Comedy of the West Indian, to which will be added High Life Below Stairs, an excellent farce. Doors will open at half past five. Admittance 25 cents.

Furnishings in the classrooms were sparse and makeshift. The desks were boxes made over, wash stands, and tea tables. Although it was a tuition school, the boys took turns after school splitting wood and sweeping out the rooms. Heat was supplied by one large and several smaller stoves.

When the Library Lyceum was built on the site of the academy, six rooms were set aside for the academy, whose students came from far and near, many later becoming leading men in social, legal, commercial, and professional activities.

The success of the Morris Academy prompted the founding of a rival institution in 1801, the Warren Academy. In 1803, the building of the Warren Academy

*Young men in Morristown through the 1800s usually attended the Morris Academy in South Street, which started in 1782 with 33 pupils. When the Lyceum purchased the school, it reserved six rooms for the school, which closed several years after fire destroyed the Lyceum.*

75

*Miss Dana's School for Young Ladies, described as a school ahead of its time, opened in 1887 on South Street in the buildings of the former Morris Female Institute. It closed in 1913.*

burned and was replaced by a new red brick building in North Park Place. After a few years, however, the school closed.

Miss Dana's school, perhaps the most progressive school in Morristown at the turn of the century, drew students from families throughout the United States, including students from families prominent in the nation's professional, government, and industrial life.

A school brochure described the school as:

> Set well back off the street with an impressive entrance drive broken by a central circular lawn circled by attractive elms, oaks, and silver birch trees. The main Victorian style school building faces the drive. Inside two curving stairways in the main hall lead to pupils double and single sleeping rooms, which boast elegantly draped windows, tidy beds, closets, dressing tables, study desks and chairs, occasional tables, and a school flag bearing the one word "Dana."
>
> Downstairs through the front hall is a large curtained parlor and library. A passage leads to the main classrooms and assembly hall. At the rear of the property is the school bakery and kitchens adjoining tennis courts and a sports field. . . .
>
> The school buildings are desirably situated and are surrounded by ample grounds permitting many out of door sports. The buildings are heated electrically and are equipped with fire escapes. The instructors in charge of departments of study are college graduates or have had special training for their work. The language classes are under the care

of a resident teacher. Additional opportunity to perfect the languages is given by talks in the dining room. The music department offers private vocal and instrumental lessons together with lessons in harmony and ensembly playing.

For the art courses a studio is provided well equipped with models and casts. The instruction includes drawing in nature and life and crayon, water color and oil. The students of history have a large collection of photographs and illustrated works of reference. Class work is supplemented by trips to the Metropolitan and other museums.

Miss Dana leased the facilities from the Morris Female Institute, which opened in 1860 as a boarding school for young ladies. One graduate remembered: "Every morning we filed into the dining room led by Miss Elizabeth Dana in her rattly silk dress. A clergyman followed in frock coat with head bowed and hands clasped on a bible."

Rules were very strict. Parents had to send monthly allowances by check. At month's end, each boarder had to present neatly balanced books accounting for the money received. Eating between meals was banned. Candy was not allowed. Students could go for afternoon drives with female friends as chaperons with written permission from their parents. Without permission, a coachman was required.

Students were advised to bring little jewelry to school. Evening dresses were banned. Parents were urged not to provide their daughters with low-neck dresses.

The first graduating class was in 1891; the last in 1912, one year before the school closed following Miss Dana's death. The buildings were then occupied by the Randolph Military Academy from 1912 to 1915.

The Peck School traces its history to 1891 when Miss Christine D. Sutphen opened a primary school for six girls in her home at 22 Franklin Place at the request of the students' parents. She retired in 1917 and Lorraine T. Peck, after whom the school is named, became the principal owner. In 1918, after a few years at the YMCA, he changed the name of the school to the Peck School and purchased the Abell-Taintor property at 11 Elm Street, building a substantial addition and remodeling the house to accommodate grades K-9.

Increased enrollment soon made it necessary to seek additional quarters and he leased the house at 21 Franklin Street, moving the girls' department there.

In 1947, the school purchased "Lindenwold," the 10-acre South Street estate of John Claflin, one of the foremost dry goods merchants in the world. Renovations and remodeling of the ivy-covered stone mansion and grounds commenced at once with additions added to the mansion in 1955 and 1959.

Noted Alumni of Peck School included former Congressman Peter H.B. Frelinghuysen; Reverend Paul Moore, former Episcopal Bishop of New York; author and photographer Jill Krementz; and harpist Daphne Shih. These and other pupils went on to secondary schools, including Kent Place, Pingry, Oak Knoll, and Villa Walsh.

The Morristown School on the Whippany Road was founded by three men, Francis C. Woodman, Thomas Brown Jr., and Arthur P. Butler, who came to Morristown to teach in another school. When that school closed, the three men took over St. Bartholomew's School in 1896 and changed the name to the Morristown School.

Recognized as an Ivy League prep school and a feeder school for Harvard University, the school benefited from donations of Morristown's millionaires, several of whom served on its board of trustees. Grinnell Willis, perhaps Morristown's leading philanthropist, donated funds in 1910 to renovate two dormitories in the main building and for a headmaster's house, plus $20,000 the following year to erect a gymnasium.

In 1915, the 22-acre Desidero tract opposite the school, part of the former Julius Catlin estate, was donated to the school by Woodbury C. Landon, a Morristown millionaire and school trustee. Named the Landon house in his honor, the Desidero mansion was used for a number of years to house lower grades. When hit by the Depression in the early 1930s, however, the school was forced to sell the tract to a family who sold it to the Desideros.

In 1919, a few parents raised $10,000 to purchase the Washer farm between the school and the Whippany River, an action that increased the campus size to accommodate the rising enrollment, which tripled in the first five years the school was in operation.

In 1961, new classrooms were built in keeping with the Colonial architecture of the school buildings. Included were two special classrooms, four regular classrooms, and four one-bedroom apartments for faculty members.

Ten years later, in 1971, the all boys school became co-ed after merging with the Beard School founded in Orange in 1891. Allen P. Kirby Jr., president of the board of trustees, announced that the school would forego its five-day boarding program to make room for a co-ed schedule and would change its name to the Morristown-Beard School.

In April 1975, the school once again got a chance to acquire the Desidero property, then owned by the former Allied Chemical Corporation, which had purchased it in 1968 for use while its world headquarters was under construction on the nearby estate of Otto H. Kahn. Phillip Anderson, headmaster, said the addition of the Dersidero property would double the campus size and provide for long range expansion plans. The New Jersey State Highway Department, however, would not approve plans for an elevated walkway over Whippany Road and the plan was dropped.

Enterprising students built and operated their own radio station, WMSR, at the school in 1962 to provide music, news, and weather reports from 4 p.m. to 10:30 p.m. five days a week.

In 1984, ground was broken for the William E. Simon gymnasium and the William W. Rooke family swimming pool, named in their honor because they were the largest contributors to a $7.7-million fundraising campaign. Two years later, plans were approved by Morris Township for a 250-seat cafeteria, six additional classrooms, three science laboratories, a computer room, and renovation of the south wing of the main building.

The most famous alumnus of the school was John Reed, a Communist and journalist, best known as the author of *Ten Days That Shook the World*, a classic chronicle of the Russian revolution. As a tribute to his role in the revolution, he was buried under the Kremlin Wall, not far from the tomb of Lenin. Other prominent graduates included Chapman Grant, grandson of President Ulysses S. Grant; Jacqueline Kennedy's father John W. Bouvier III and his brother William; Charles Morton, associate editor of the *Atlantic Monthly*; and Roger Burlingame, editor of *Scribners Magazine*.

St. Hilda School, conducted by the Deaconesses of the Episcopal Church, purchased the Avenue House, a 60-room hotel at the corner of Washington Street and Western Avenue in 1886. They immediately fenced the property (site of the former Morristown YMCA) with a board fence, building a chapel and later a three-story frame building connected to the hotel building by a covered passageway.

Specialized private schools, their classes limited in size, advertised for pupils in the *Palladium of Liberty*. Typical were those of a Mr. Barthelemy, who taught French and English at the Warren Academy; a Mr. Martin who opened a school for French in 1808; and a Mr. Duncan, who operated an evening school teaching reading, writing, arithmetic, and Italian bookkeeping (most likely, bookkeeping in Italian).

Other private schools in Morristown included the Morris Female Institute on South Street, the Young Ladies' School, Miss Bostwick's School for Young Ladies, Sisters of St. John the Baptist School, and a Roman Catholic School, all on Maple Avenue.

*The Morristown School on the Whippany Road was founded by three teachers who took over St. Bartholomew's School in 1896 and changed the name to the Morristown School. In 1971, it merged with the all-girls Beard School and kept the Beard name.*

On opening day, December 13, 1869, more than 400 students aged 5 to 18 from Morristown and Morris Township were admitted to Morristown's first public school on Maple Avenue. The three-story red brick structure was built on a 1.8-acre tract donated by George Cobb, Morristown's first mayor (1865–1870) who made his fortune in the New York iron business. He also donated $10,000 to help defray the cost of construction. The building had 12 classrooms, a recitation room, cloakrooms, and a third floor auditorium. A large coal burning furnace heated the school.

Ten teachers taught the students, most doing double duty in upper and lower grades. On December 23, 1875, five young women and three young men comprised Morristown High School's first graduating class.

By 1910, the school was overcrowded and outmoded with more than 800 students despite an addition built in 1893 and construction of two other grade schools in Morristown: one on Speedwell Avenue, now the American Legion Post, and the other on Mill Street, now headquarters for the school administration and board of education.

The flood of students increased each year. To accommodate them, a second addition was added to the Maple Avenue School in 1911. The tremendous increase in students was attributed in part to more and more out of town high school students registering at Morristown High School, many of whom rode trains, trolley cars, and horse-drawn coaches from Brookside, Mendham, Denville, Morris Plains, Stirling, New Vernon, and Gillette.

*Morristown's first public school was built on Maple Avenue in 1869 on land donated by George Cobb, Morristown's first mayor, who made his fortune in the New York iron business. He also donated $10,000 to help defray construction costs.*

Mothers representing the Civic Association and the Women's Town Improvement Society in 1912 proposed construction of a new high school with an auditorium, gymnasium, rooms for industrial and domestic science classes, and bright airy classrooms. They further proposed as a site the 5.4-acre Noble tract at the corner of Early Street and Atno Avenue. Their proposal was approved by the voters October 9, 1914 after further expansion of the Maple Avenue School was voted down.

The Noble property was condemned and purchased by the board of education for $10,000 in January 1915. The cornerstone for the new high school facing Early Street was laid the following September 9. The brick building was ready for classes in September 1918. The initial enrollment totaled 718 students. Cost of the school was $335,000.

Suburbia engulfed the greater Morristown area after World War II, swept along by the GI Bill that guaranteed World War II veterans low cost mortgages. Slowly, farmers' pastures and orchards blossomed with housing developments, putting pressure on boards of education to create new K-12 districts or unite with other districts in creating new regional schools.

Students from out of town districts began enrolling in either the new Morris Knolls or Morris Hills Regional High School districts. Morris Township joined Morristown in 1971 as a full school partner. At the same time, Harding Township withdrew its pupils and sent them to Madison High School, leaving Morris Plains as the only sending district.

The Morristown Board of Education in 1955 notified the Morris Township Board of Education that because of the high enrollment and limited facilities, Morris Township students would not be accepted after September, 1958. The action touched off 17 years of bitter, costly legal maneuvering and a series of township referendums seeking construction of a separate township high school.

After the 1955 rejection as the furor over a separate township high school mounted, township students were scheduled to be sent to Madison High School. In 1961, however, the township accepted a truce and brought students back to Morristown High School while the series of legal battles increased.

Finally, in 1971, the New Jersey Supreme Court ruled to prevent the township from withdrawing its students from Morristown High School and ordered a merger of Morristown and Morris Township secondary school systems into what became known as the Morris School District.

In the meantime, Morristown began a program to enlarge its elementary schools. Almost every year from 1951 through 1958, a major addition or new school was opened. In 1951, the George Washington School was tripled in size; in 1954, a new Thomas Jefferson School opened; in 1955, a six classroom addition was added to the Alexander Hamilton School; in 1956, the Lafayette School was tripled in size; and in 1958, additions were added to the Thomas Jefferson and the high schools.

Two new wings were added to the high school to accommodate the growing number of students, some of whom were dissatisfied with the class scheduling, while some white students expressed anger over what they felt was an attitude of preferential treatment of African-American students by the administration.

Seething tempers among the students boiled over on May 6, 1974, resulting in a full-scale riot at the high school. The majority of students, both black and white, left the building and either walked home or called their parents to come and get them.

After the riots, the school was closed most of the following week because of the fighting between several hundred of the school's 2,400 students. Eight were injured, two by chemical mace. When the school reopened, strict security measures were imposed, including a police community-relations specialist assigned to the school, policemen in civilian clothing stationed inside and outside the building, and mandatory ID checks of all students entering the school.

One college, St. Elizabeth's, was founded in the greater Morristown area in the dusk of the 1800s. It was the first women's college in New Jersey and the first Catholic women's college in the United States.

Almost half a century later, in 1933, the Morris Junior College, the forerunner of the County College of Morris, opened its doors to students in Randolph Township. It was followed in 1958 by Fairleigh Dickinson University, which purchased the 110-room Hamilton McKown Twombly mansion on Madison Avenue for its Madison campus.

The County College of Morris, a two-year institution that opened its doors in 1968, is funded by the state, the Board of Chosen Freeholders, and tuition. It offers curricula leading to associate degrees. Both day and evening, full and part-time classes are offered, and are constantly expanding in scope to meet the needs of county residents.

The College of St. Elizabeth, founded in 1899, has its roots in the Academy of St. Elizabeth, established 40 years earlier. When it began in 1860, the Academy (the name "convent" came later) shared the Benjamin Pierson residence on Park Avenue, Madison with a small group of Sisters of Charity who had established a permanent Mother House and a boys' academy, Seton Hall. When the boys' school moved to South Orange in 1859, Mother Xavier Mehegan purchased the property. Between 1860 and 1899, more farmland in the area was acquired, enlarging the campus to more than 400 acres, and the center section of the large brick administration building, Xavier Hall, was built.

The initial class of five girls entered the college in 1899, receiving the first degrees granted women in New Jersey in 1903. To meet the numerical needs of the growing college, Santa Rita Hall, with facilities for housing 105 students, was built in 1907. From that date, construction of additional facilities was always underway. A chapel was dedicated in 1909. A plant experiment house to meet the needs of the botany department opened in 1912, followed by Santa Maria Hall in 1913, and the Greek Theater in 1932. Other buildings followed, including Nevin Hall, a 14-room residence for seniors in the home economics department, and two separate laboratory structures.

In 1999, the Century Plan celebrating the 100th anniversary of the college was launched. Designed as a comprehensive plan, it called for campus renewal and a

*The College of St. Elizabeth, the first woman's college in New Jersey and the first Catholic women's college in the United States, was founded in 1899, 40 years after the Academy of St. Elizabeth opened its doors in Convent.*

multi-million-dollar construction and renovation program designed to reshape and revitalize the physical environment. Included was a new administration building, classrooms, library, residential, recreational, and general facilities to meet the projected enrollment growth in undergraduate and adult continuing education programs.

At the close of the Civil War, the Morris and Essex Railroad station, through the efforts of Mother Xavier, was moved to its present site so students and staff would not have to travel by horse and carriage from the Madison station. A new wooden station was built by Mother Xavier, who for a time paid the stationmaster's salary. The present brick structure dates to 1913. It was purchased from the railroad in 1966 by Morris Township for $12,000 and renovated.

The area became known as Convent Station in 1876. Twenty years later, in 1896, the Sisters of Charity deeded Convent Avenue, leading from the station to Madison Avenue, to Morris Township.

In 1925, the Benedictine monks of Saint Mary's Abbey acquired for $155,000 a 380-acre parcel of the 4,000-acre estate of Luther Kountze, founder and head of the New York Branch of the banking firm of Kountze Brothers at 270 Mendham Road, after his heirs foreclosed on two other purchases.

In 1939, the monks opened Delbarton School, an independent college preparatory day and boarding school for boys. At first, activities centered about "Old Main," the white granite mansion with walls 3 feet thick that Kountze built in 1888 overlooking Washington Valley, and the carriage house, which later burned. Eventually, a 21-classroom building, living quarters for students, 6 tennis courts, 6 athletic fields, and 21 faculty housing units for the teachers were built.

The school quickly achieved prominence, winning a contest honoring excellence among 60 of the nation's secondary schools.

In 1938, the $2.5-million Saint Mary's Abbey was built on a knoll behind Old Main to provide living quarters for 37 monks, 12 novices, and 40 clerics. During World War II, the basement of the abbey was classified as a fallout shelter.

In 1930, another of the great mansions overlooking Washington Valley, that of Samuel H. Gillespie on Picatinny Road, was opened as Villa Walsh Academy, a private college preparatory and finishing school for girls. Staffed by the Religious Teachers of St. Lucy Filippini, the 131-acre campus purchased for $125,000 by the religious order was first called Villa Lucia.

Classes are held in a building constructed in the late 1960s, which includes laboratories, classrooms, and a convertible gym-auditorium that seats 1,000.

Villa Walsh College, whose primary purpose was to prepare young sisters to teach in Catholic schools, was opened to all young women in 1970 with special emphasis on a unique non-sectarian service volunteer program. It was closed to lay students the following year.

An attraction of the campus is the 70-foot-high tower built by Gillespie in 1894 over a 417-foot-deep well. Its picture has appeared on more postcards mailed from Morristown than any other scene. From its top on a clear day, one can see the Brooklyn Bridge.

*Villa Walsh Academy is located in the Samuel H. Gillespie mansion on Picatinny Road, bought by the Religious Teachers of St. Lucy Filippi in 1930 for $125,000.*

# 5. An Inland Newport

The story of the Gilded Age in Morristown, its rise and demise, is an analysis of how fabulously wealthy nineteenth-century family founders, those individuals who were the most successful and stood at the head of the functional class hierarchy, lived, worked, and played. These were the decision makers in the political, economic, and military spheres as well as the leaders in law, engineering, medicine, education, finance, religion, and the arts.

This narrative traces the dramatic rise and fortunes of America's millionaires during the nation's Gilded Age when the tiny village of Morristown, New Jersey became the core of the richest and least-known colony of wealthy people in the world.

It is a factual saga of people caught up in the flood of the most overwhelming accumulation of wealth the United States has ever witnessed, told as it happened; muddled, enabling, disgraceful, frustrating, full of a greatness that will never reappear in this country or anywhere else.

Here is presented not only the drama and pathos of a great sweep of events, but also the many illuminating sidelights, oddities, and amusing trifles, all of which go to make up a full picture of the Morristown created by and for these millionaire barons of industry between 1880 and the Depression of 1929.

The twilight of the nineteenth century produced the beginnings of the famous plutocracy whose handsome mansions once lined Morristown's South Street and Madison Avenue, aptly termed "The Great White Way." As the years passed, the vast land holdings of these men and women of wealth spilled over to Normandy Heights, Washington Valley, Mendham, Morris Plains, and Madison.

"If you choose to be at the railroad station at Morristown, New Jersey at about five o'clock of any weekday afternoon, you will see one of the comedies of real life, a comedy of almost pathetic seriousness to the participants, yet absorbingly interesting and almost mirth provoking to the spectator." With these words, a New York newspaper writer at the turn of the century described the arrival home from offices in New York of the barons of industry, financiers, and business tycoons who comprised Morristown's elaborate country society of the Gilded Age.

He wrote of handsome equipages filling nearby streets, automobiles lined up on the station grounds, and public hacks crowded along the curbs:

*Florham, the undisputed center of Morris County's social life, was built by Hamilton Mckown Twombly in 1896. The 110-room mansion in Madison Avenue is a replica of one wing of Henry VIII's Hampton Court Palace. It survives today as the Madison campus of Fairleigh Dickinson University.*

Liveried flunkeys are everywhere, many sitting stiff and unseeing on the seat of a fashionable trap; others standing like automatons beside the emblazoned doors of heavy broughams.

It is time for the arrival of the Millionaires Express and everyone is on the qui viva of expectancy. In a moment the train will be in and then all will be hustle and bustle.

Suddenly the bell announcing the approach of the train begins to ring. The gate tenders lower the crossing gates that warn traffic of the imminent arrival of the train. And in a puffing of smoke, clanging of bells, and gleaming of polished brass, engine 100 pulls into the station platform.

From the forward coaches an indiscriminate mass of humanity pours forth, but from the club coaches at the rear emerge in leisurely fashion a silk-tied and unusually corpulent host, men who perhaps have spent the day considering the fate of nations, the financing of a new transcontinental railroad or the funding of a dog show or monkey dinner.

Hamilton McKown Twombly, a man worth at least $70 million, makes his way to the drag-and-four where his daughter, Miss Ruth Twombly, awaits him surrounded by a coachman, two footmen and a postilion. Richard A. McCurdy, the president of the Mutual Life Insurance Co., walks slowly to his splendid Victoria, where awaits Mrs. McCurdy, a coachman and a footman. Luther Kountze enters his eight horsepower Panhard, to be whirred away to his palace on the Mendham Road. Robert H. McCurdy hurries to his pale blue motor car; William Slack Letchford to his trap; Otto H. Kahn to his saddle horse; John I. Waterbury to his brougham, and in a few minutes they are all speeding away to nearby mansions.

These descriptive words written at the height of Morristown's popularity as a center for the wealthy tell much of the Morristown that was, of the men and women who created a unique country retreat, their modes and style of life.

As early as 1886, a newspaper article mentions that the posh cars of the "Royal Blood," as the Millionaires Express was initially tabbed, were palaces: roomy, easy riding, and light with paneled walls, carpeted floors, and wicker chairs.

It also noted that two public hacks awaited the arrival of the train and were patronized by the "swells." By the early 1890s, however, society with its protocol and code had taken over. Nobody who was anybody would be caught dead in a public taxi at the railroad station. Second only to the 31-minute train ride to Hoboken and the side-wheeled ferry boat that crossed the Hudson River was how these men of wealth arrived at the depot for the Millionaires Express at 8:25 a.m. each weekday.

Take, for instance, James T. Pyle of Mount Kemble Avenue, who made his pile in Pyle's Pearline, one of the early detergents. His coach would drive up to the railroad station at a brisk trot, Pyle in the driver's seat. As the carriage reached the station, coachman and groom would jump down smartly and wait while Pyle made a rapid change from his white driving duster into his New York jacket and dashed for the club car.

Each carriage had its own special waiting place at the station plaza, with the most elite in the most convenient spots. Recalls one Morristown resident: "If you appropriated one of these sacred locations, you'd find a polite groom at your elbow touching his hat and asking if you'd mind moving over a bit."

"Talk about drag racing," another old timer said. "The commuters wearing trim beards and the formal business suits of the day used to take off hell-bent for leather up Elm Street or toward The Green, driving so close to each other and so fast that they often came within scant inches of shearing off a wheel."

The more athletic types marched off to the Morristown Club, then located at 126 South Street, which for many was a way-station in their journey homeward. Here they continued where they'd left off in the club car, at cards, conversation, or something stronger.

The story noted that Morristown:

Is the city of millionaires and there is not another community like it in the United States, possibility not in the world. Here are gathered together in one little circle with a radius of three miles, more men of millions than can be found elsewhere the country over. Between 90 and 100 plutocrats live here, and with their servants, retainers and small trade people, who serve them, make up a town of 12,000 inhabitants.

It is a city of handsome dwellings, beautiful palaces and country mansions, some of which have cost millions of dollars to erect and equip. There is "Florham," for instance, the country seat of the Twomblys where in the center of a park of 160 acres devoted entirely to lawns and flower gardens stands a mansion of 110 rooms. Adjoining this park is "Florham Farms" of 750 acres, on which Mr. Twombly indulges his penchant for farming and plays the country squire.

Here too is the riding academy in a great building with a tanbark floor where the Twombly youngsters were taught that graceful seat which earned them so much praise at metropolitan horse shows, and where their horses where put through high school tactics of the advanced order. At "Florham," Senator and Mrs. Chauncey Depew are frequent visitors and it was here that the Dutchess of Marlborough was entertained.

But the Twombly place is but one of a dozen or more establishments of the same kind. At "Delbarton," the Kountze place on the Mendham Road, is the same thing except that the architecture is Elizabethan. It is at the latter place that the Vanderbilt and Gerry boys and others of their set in New York are frequent visitors.

"Cedar Court," the country seat of the Kahns is a vast park of 1,100 acres surrounding a Moorish style palace of 60 rooms erected in 1900 on one of the most prominent sites in Morris Township. Here all of the architecture is of the Moorish-Italian style and the general atmosphere of the property is that of a French estate.

Other estates include "Giralda Farms," the 1-square-mile estate of Geraldine Rockefeller Dodge, who at her death in 1973 left an estate of $101 million; John I. Waterbury's Elizabethan mansion at Convent; George Marshall Allen's "Glynallan," modeled after "Compton Wyngates," an English manor house built in 1528; John H. Claflin's "Lindenwold," a 24-room Victorian granite mansion set amidst a 175-acre estate; Seth Thomas's 27-room "Red Gate" mansion in Harding Township, the site of New Year's Day banquets of the 400; William V.S. Thorne's "Gateways," a 30-room, $400,000 Georgian-style mansion; "Glen Alpine," the 50-acre estate of David H. McAlpin, a tobacco magnate; "Alnwick Hall," the huge yellow-brick castle mansion of General Edward P. Meany; and "Delbarton," the 4,000-acre estate of Luther Kountze.

Other millionaires who called the greater Morristown area their summer home included Richard A. McCurdy, president of the Mutual Life Insurance Company; Robert F. Ballantine, president of P. Ballantine and Sons brewery; John A. Stewart, organizer and president of the United States Trust Company and financial advisor

*Delbarton, the mansion of New York banker Luther Kountze, was built from granite quarried on the 4,000-acre estate in 1880 on Route 24. Today, it is Delbarton Preparatory School.*

to President Abraham Lincoln; Charles W. Armour, New York investment broker; Eugene S. Higgins, a capitalist termed the "richest and handsomest bachelor in New York in 1898"; Harry E. Niese, the "Dean of Sugar Refiners;" Dr. Frederick H. Humphreys, president of the Humphreys Homeopathic Medicine Company; Charles Scribner, president of Charles Scribner's and Sons, publishers; and Frederick R. Kellogg, one of the most prominent corporation counsels in the United States.

The rapid accumulation of wealth was due in principal to the way the new breed of American gentry felt about their country and its place in the world. Bursting progress and the confidence that the future held both fame and fortune was reflected in every millionaire, whether a veteran or a budding newcomer to the ranks of the rich.

Mark Twain, a frequent visitor at Morristown mansions, explained it thus: "Nearly every man has his dream, his pet scheme, whereby he is to advance himself socially or pecuniarily."

Historian Henry Adams, a great-grandson of President John Adams, found that the average New Yorker "was a pushing, energetic, ingenious person, always awake and trying to get ahead of his neighbors."

James B. Duke, the founder of the American Tobacco Company, expressed his ideology more bluntly. He wrote, "First hit your enemies in the pocketbook, hit 'em hard, then you either buy them out or take them in with you."

The initial edition of the *Morristown Social Directory*, the Blue Book of society's 400 published in 1896, eight years after the idea of the social register was born in New York, contained the names of 537 persons, including 54 millionaires with a total wealth of $289 million. Two years later, in the 1898 edition, 79 new names of millionaires were added.

It was a day of licensed piracy, a great evasion of taxation, exploitation of the poor, and profiteering from gigantic thefts. The class that had the money—no matter how that money was obtained, irrespective of how much fraud or sacrifice of life attended its accumulation—stood out with a luminous distinctness. It arrogated to itself all that was superior and it enacted and was invested with a lordly deference.

It was a day of prosperity, all industry was tending toward concentration, and more and more money was flowing into the hands of fewer and fewer men like the Vanderbilts, Twomblys, Rockefellers, and Dodges. The iniquities of that system were not only defined, they were sanctioned. The economists preached that classlessness and equality were evil, and by and large people believed them. Rise early, strive, save—those were the virtues of the day.

A new era of splendor had set in. Observing the social scene in Morristown, residents were amazed by the magnificence of the mansions being built and the costliness of the festivities and the fashions. To many, the quiet farming community they had known suddenly seemed a town of crowds and carnival—breezy, recklessly extravagant, perpetually bent on pleasure.

The glow of the incandescent light suddenly appeared to illuminate the homes of the very rich, replacing gas and kerosene as a source of light. To provide the

*The Fairfield House was built by John I. Waterbury, president of the Manhattan Trust Company, on a 60-acre tract on Madison Avenue in 1901. It was razed in 1941 for housing development.*

electricity for this new form of illumination, millionaires like Hamilton McKown Twombly, who married a Vanderbilt; Charles H. Mellon, New York investment broker; and Charles W. Harkness, the third-largest holder of Standard Oil stock in the world, erected their own generating plants on their estates.

During the season, in the spring and fall months when the wealthy were in residence, the train station at Morristown became a social center each weekday morning and evening as the plush Millionaires Express departed and arrived, bringing the barons of industry and finance to and from offices in New York. It was not only the men. The wives and daughters who met them displayed the latest in fashion, often eying a neighbor's carriage with the thought "we've got to get a better one."

Some like Twombly and Richard A. McCurdy, president of the Mutual Life Insurance Company, had their own private railroad cars kept on siding on their estates. Others like Otto H. Kahn, senior partner of Kahn, Loeb & Company, hired a pullman car just to take their families to the city for a day.

The Morris County Golf Club, the Morristown Field Club, the Whippany River Club, and an exclusive haven for men only—the Morristown Club—were rallying points for entertainment, all founded by and for the enjoyment of this new breed of aristocracy. Polo, first played on a field at the Gustav Kissel estate in Washington Valley, and the fox hunt became popular pastimes that drew thousands of spectators.

To satisfy their whims, some of these blue bloods had their own private golf courses; others their own polo fields and stables of polo ponies, tennis, squash courts, and racetracks. Some, like Eugene Higgins, a capitalist, even had grandstands for the spectators.

Ex-presidents like Ulysses S. Grant; famous authors like Mark Twain, Bret Harte, and Frank Stockton; the notorious Floradora chorus sextette, which overnight became more illustrious than any other stars of the musical stage; and John L. Sullivan, the world heavyweight boxing champion, were drawn to Morristown both as residents and guests at its mansions.

The Morristown at the turn of the century, both as a community and countryside, was being changed by these men and women of wealth, changed to meet their needs and lifestyle. They founded local preparatory schools and libraries; philharmonic, chess, Shakespeare, whist, and choral clubs; and served as presidents and directors of the Morristown banks established to meet their needs.

In the summer months, the wealthy who kept fast pacers and trotters exercised them on South Street, still a dirt road, often racing each other. The practice eventually became the subject of sermons in several churches and led to the founding of the South Street racetrack made famous in Currier and Ives prints.

Coaching became one of the most elegant diversions of the elite. To achieve celebrity as an amateur whip was a consuming ambition of middle-aged "swells" and the younger set. It led to competition with the fast pacers and trotters on South Street where coach-and-fours became a common sight racing to the racetrack (now the Seton Hackney County Park).

The Honorable William Paterson, a judge who grew up on what became the Howland estate on James Street, vividly expressed the dramatic change in Morristown witnessed in the dusk of the nineteenth century in a poem entitled "Morristown," which he penned in 1894.

> And Villas Crown The Rising Hilltops Round,
> And Stately Mansions Stand Adorned with Art,
> And Liveried Coaches Roll with Rambling Sound
> Where Once Jogged On The Wagon Wheel and Cart.

The wealthy installed that new-fangled invention "the talking box," as the telephone was first known, in their homes, prompting the stringing of miles of wire on the crossarms of towering poles lining the main thoroughfares, The Green, and country roads alike.

It was not unusual for guests at the Morristown mansions to be entertained by the stars of the entertainment world, many imported in special trains for the occasion. They ranged from opera stars, musicians, and entire orchestras to vaudeville performers, noted lecturers, drama groups, and world famous sporting figures.

Expense was no consideration in this heyday of big spending. Money flowed like water to procure both the practical and the impractical in entertainment, the finest available throughout the United States and the world.

Alma Gluck, Efrem Zimbalist, Lillian Russell, Kate Claxon, Lily Langtry, Jan Paderawski, Fritz Kreisler, Mark Twain, Dr. Henry Ward Beecher, Giovanni Martinelli, the entire Metropolitan Opera, and Lucrezia Bori were guests at these elaborate functions that defied the imagination, but failed to dent the pocketbooks of Morristown's wealthy.

Leading all events for color and magnificence were the weekend house parties at the Twombly estate, the subscription dances, costume balls, society weddings, fox hunt breakfasts, New Year's Eve parties, and cotillions. To them came European nobility, leaders in the fields of business, politics, and the arts, and members of the 400.

Any excuse provided a reason to entertain. The only decision to be made by the host and hostess was the form the entertainment would take and the guest list.

General and Mrs. Edward P. Meany planned elaborate events "just because they wanted to have a musical"; the Twomblys threw a noted barn dance to celebrate the completion of a $75,000 stable complex; the George Marshall Allens, a house party to utilize scenery imported from France; and Mrs. Richard A. McCurdy, a garden party to introduce to Morristown society a noted Spanish dance troupe then the rave of New York.

Mrs. Meany had a great enthusiasm for music. Her patronage of the Metropolitan Opera was acknowledged by the conductor, Adolph L. Rothmeyer, who composed the "Alnwick Hall March" to honor both her and her estate on Madison Avenue.

Mrs. Meany was not only a leader in Morristown's swagger set, but also in New York City and in Washington, where in 1902 she was hostess at a gala reception given by Vice President and Mrs. James S. Sherman in honor of the diplomatic corps, and at Hot Springs, Virginia, a center for southern society where the Meanys and many other millionaires from Morristown wintered.

She was a frequently seen figure on Madison Avenue when she took her daily walk. Following 30 feet behind her was an imported car, open in front with an enclosed rear, driven by a chauffeur, and attended by a liveried footman "just in case she tired."

When the Twomblys issued gilt-edged invitations to their now famous barn dance on November 30, 1891, hundreds of persons with names like Vanderbilt, Whitney, McCurdy, Frelinghuysen, Vernam, and Kip accepted. It was no ordinary affair. A newspaper account of the event described it as "one of the most beautiful and unique entertainments ever given in Morristown or indeed in New Jersey."

More than 300 guests from Morris County and the metropolis danced on a 250-foot-long hardwood floor guarded by rows of columns twined with ropes of evergreens, sheaves of wheat, and red, white, and blue pampas grass. On one wall, a plow was draped with rhododendron ropes. Everywhere were garlands of dried corn on the cob and pumpkins, each containing a tiny incandescent lamp.

*Alnwick Hall, a yellow brick, Tudor-style castle on Madison Avenue, was built in 1911 by General Edward P. Meany, counsel for the American Telegraph and Telephone Company. His parties were famous.*

*Mrs. Ethel Geraldine Rockefeller Dodge, last of the great dowagers of an all but forgotten society, kneels here with Rin Tin Tin, the German shepherd movie and television star, at her estate Giralda Farms. The 1-mile-square estate is now an office park.*

Overhead, 2,000 tiny electric lights installed at a cost of $6,000 gleamed like stars. Just in case the temperamental incandescents gave out, however, a system of calcium lights was mounted on a platform in the middle of the floor. The hostess received her guests behind a Japanese screen in the bull stable, which for the occasion was furnished as a parlor.

At midnight, supper was served in another room, the walls of which were draped with bunting. Electric lights were everywhere. Scattered about the room were little tables and on each was a pumpkin hollowed out to hold flowers. From their midst rose a slender candlestick with a red, yellow, or pink shade to match the colors of the flowers from the Twombly's greenhouses.

The next day, the regular occupants of the barn were ushered in: the Twombly herd of Guernsey cattle, described by *Country Gentleman*, a leading agriculture magazine of the day, as "the finest in the nation." Their milk, it is said, was peddled in the nearby towns of Madison, Chatham, Convent, and Summit from a $1,200 wagon drawn by a pair of matched thoroughbred horses worth $1,500 wearing silver-mounted harnesses.

It was the debutante ball, the traditional "Coming Out" dance for the daughters of the wealthy, however, that drew the cream of society to the Lyceum and Washington Hall, the two major ballrooms in Morristown frequented by the 400 at the turn of the century. Typical was the year 1890 when the dames of society, magnificent in their finest apparel, vied to eclipse one another.

One by one, the debutantes, bedecked with glittering jewels, descended the great staircase to make their debut into high society. Each was gowned in exquisite taste: white tulle with French lace and ribbons, pink chiffon, yellow brocaded satin, and the faintest shades of blue and dark green velvet.

Ropes of greens and autumn foliage festooned all sides of the ballroom. Large plants and towering palms concealed the musicians. Tiny electric lamps, the globes covered with pink gauze, hung from the gallery railings and boxes. Luxurious sofas were tucked in out-of-the-way corners.

The grand dames of the reception committee led the applause. Included were Mrs. Joseph Revere, Mrs. Hamilton McKown Twombly, Mrs. Stephen Whitney, Mrs. Albert H. Vernam, Mrs. Gustav Kissel, Mrs. Louis Thebaud, and Mrs. William Shippen.

Eight dances were given each year at Washington Hall, sometimes referred to as McAlpin Hall (located on the site of the Century 21 Department Store). Three balls, with supper, continued until 2 or 3 a.m. The other five affairs were less formal, usually terminating at midnight.

An invitation to these balls was proof positive of good standing among the millionaires and the society they bred. Wilburn F. Day Jr., son of Morristown's internationally recognized caterer of the Gilded Age, recalled, "There were no hangers on at the fringes of society in Morristown as so often was the case elsewhere in the country. Either you were in or you were out."

One winter cotillion at the Lyceum was made famous by a prank of Eugene Higgins, termed New York's most eligible bachelor and a millionaire used to shocking the staid and proper matrons of Morristown society. He brought the dancers and musicians to an abrupt halt when from the balcony he tossed what appeared to be a beautiful blond onto the dance floor. The dancing couples froze, backing off in shock until they realized it was only a dummy.

It was at the Lyceum that Richard A. McCurdy gave his famous ball in 1900, which carried a price tab of between $50,000 and $75,000—the exact amount never having been made public. For the event, the three-story building was transformed into a veritable fairy palace with cost apparently the least figure of consideration. An extra dance floor was constructed over the seats in the large hall. The ballroom's fluted columns were draped with grapevines, which concealed taps from which eight different types of imported wines flowed when guests pressed a button. Small tables in an improvised tapestry-draped dining room were piled high with goodies ranging from glazed partridge to quail and bon bons.

The front and entrance to the Lyceum was festooned with electric lights. Other strings of incandescent bulbs were draped across South Street to flash numbers, which when illuminated was the signal for waiting coachmen and carriages to report to the Lyceum's front door. Every fixture bespoke the luxury of the very rich, from gold-engraved invitations, each hand delivered, to the liveried flunkies and elaborate gowns of the grande dames.

Morristown residents who were at first amazed by the magnificence of the mansions and the costliness of the festivities and fashions that they bred, slowly gave way to accept the new era of splendor, absurd extravagance, and the emergence of a cult of elegance spawned by wealth.

For Morristown the dawn of the Gilded Age meant a farewell to simplicity. A new era of splendor had set in. For the wealthy, the need to maintain a charming pace imposed an unflagging effort. Rivalry was no less real for being ceremonious. It didn't matter whether it was a successful party, the food and the caterers who served it outstanding, or the entertainment unique. Each society matron had to have something just a little bit better, and in many cases just a little more costly, than her neighbor.

The changing landscape was vividly outlined in one newspaper account shortly after the turn of the century. Reporting on millionaires' plans for the coming season, it stated:

> The Charles W. Harknesses of 685 Fifth Avenue, New York, are about to open a new country house with stables, garage, gardener's cottage and a complete electric generating plant (Madison Avenue); the General Edward P. Meany's are opening drives and erecting three new (guest) residences (Madison Avenue); The Dudley Olcotts, who have recently come into $20 million, are building a Japanese garden, conservatories and palm house (Normandy Parkway); Granville M. White of Mutual Life Insurance fame is having a new residence put up in Madison Avenue; the Louis Gillespies are putting an addition to their skyrocketing residence on Picatinny Mountain; ex-governor Franklin Murphy of New Jersey is making extensive improvements on a country home on the Mendham Road, and the David H. McAlpins will soon move into the magnificent home built for them by Mrs. McAlpin's father, Benjamin F. Evans.

Social life during this glittering period was like a calling card: elegant, graceful, artificial, extremely formal, and set to a pattern. The newcomer to town, no matter what their social standing, wealth, or family name never made friendly overtures. Instead, they waited for a member of the old guard to come calling with a card in hand. The newcomer, in turn, was expected to "leave a card" at the old guard member's residence.

Ladies who planned to receive visitors sent out calling cards with a simple note written in one corner stating "At home on Tuesday afternoons." This meant that the hostess would receive callers to tea each week on that day without fail. Those who failed to comply with the social rules by which society was governed found themselves on the outside looking in no matter who they were or what wealth they had in their bank accounts.

As the mansions multiplied, many of the town residents found employment in the homes of the wealthy. Others catered to their market requirements and the expansion of town needs and services to meet the growing demands created by the increased number of estates.

One merchant recalled those days, now only memories. He was Wilbur F. Day Jr., son of the founder of the Day Catering Service, which served thousands

*Macculloch Hall, a Victorian museum on Macculloch Avenue, was built in 1822 by George Perot Macculloch, the promoter of the Morris Canal. The wing on the right was added in 1814 as a schoolhouse.*

of elite social affairs in the Gilded Age. The catering business is gone, but the memories of catering 12 weddings in one June afternoon; a $7,000 600-pound tiered wedding cake; fresh strawberries glazed in sugar, a favorite at many mansions; and receptions for 3,000 persons linger.

The architecture of the mansions these men and women of wealth erected was extremely varied, a menagerie of styles. The architects of that day displayed an innocent, delightfully free and varied character, a character motivated often by social and political ideals and not restrained by physical, financial, or practical limitations.

The Victorian style so prominent in Morristown's Gilded Age was perfect for newly successful Americans. Its simple tenant was to be original. In Morristown, it took the most diverse approaches: a collection of varied residences alike in only one respect; all were built in a motif likely to provoke a strong visual response from those seeing them. To accomplish this required a mansion to be original and to be dazzlingly picturesque.

Such was the mansion built on South Street by Richard A. McCurdy, a mansion about which one New York newspaperman wrote: "at a quick glance one would take for the Metropolitan Museum of Art or the Fontainebleau Palace." Each was different. "Delbarton," the mansion of Luther Kountze, was a copy of an English manor house; "Florham," the Hamilton McKown Twombly 110-room residence, was a copy of an English palace; and the mansion of Louis C. Gillespie overlooking Washington Valley, a southern Colonial residence.

It was the society wedding with its pomp and ceremony, however, that brought forth the cream of society in their best finery, both for the ceremony itself and the scores of dinner parties, socials, and entertainments that preceded it. A headline in *The Jerseyman*, a Morristown newspaper of 1917, told the story vividly: "Society All Agog Over Wedding."

The event was the marriage of Miss Lorraine Allen, daughter of the George Marshall Allens, leaders in Morristown and New York social circles. For the elaborate affair, Saint Peter's Episcopal Church was decorated with thousands of blooms from floor to ceiling. A screen of palms and white asters extended to the ceiling, banked with pink and blue hydrangeas. Masses of green ferns decorated the alter. The large stone columns supporting the roof were entwined with southern smilax, festoons of which were also draped from the galleries.

An understanding of the immensity of the wealth of Morristown's millionaires is further increased by the realization that a $1 bill in 1890—through inflation and devaluation—was worth $3 in 1959, $6 in 1976 and more than $10 today. Basically, this means that a country mansion that cost $500,000 to erect at the turn of the century would carry a price tag in excess of $5 million in the real estate market of today.

Eighty of these men and women of wealth who called the greater Morristown area home had only the basic qualifying $1 million; 26 had between $1 million and $10 million; and eight, between $11 million and $25 million.

A total of 37 estates were located within Morristown's municipal boundaries at the turn of the century. Here lived men both noted and feared in the business world of their day, men whose very word or iron fist could launch a multi-million-dollar project or cause a business empire to crumble. Included were

*Glynallyn, a reproduction of Compton Wyngates, a sixteenth-century English manor, was built in 1914 by George Marshall Allen, president of the George M. Allen Publishing Company on Canfield Road, Convent.*

Robert D. Foote, a banker and one-time owner of the Whippany Paperboard Company; Abner W. Colgate of the firm that still bears his name; Admiral Philip Henry Cooper, superintendent of the United States Naval Academy from 1894 to 1898; Samuel S. Dennis, president of the Howard Savings Institute in Newark and the New Jersey Railway and Canal Company; George F. Stone, a director of many railroads and banks; Gustav E. Kissel, whose wife was the granddaughter of Commodore Cornelius Vanderbilt; Peter H.B. Frelinghuysen Sr., described in 1930 as "the perfect example of the country gentleman in modern America," and Jesse Leeds Eddy and Joseph B. Dickson, both coal magnates.

Unlike the estates in areas surrounding Morristown, these men of wealth, with few exceptions, erected their mansions on small tracts of land ranging from 1 to 15 acres in size. Only five estates were larger, averaging 40 to 50 acres in size and extending into Morris Township,.

The best known beverage in Morristown in the early 1900s was Mrs. George Marshall Allen's eggnog served only once each year on New Year's Day. It was so rich and thick that it literally could be eaten with a spoon. She began to make her pièce de résistance the first week in December. The recipe was her secret and she rigorously supervised every stage of preparation, allowing the cooks to perform only stipulated functions. First the eggs had to be brown. She herself separated each of the dozens used. A cook then helped beat the whites, with Mrs. Allen making sure it was done right. Whiskey. rum, and brandy were added in exact amounts with spices and the heavy cream that came from "Twin Oaks," the estate of Peter H.B. Frelinghuysen.

The eggnog was made and stored in gallon crocks in a special upstairs room where the windows remained open even in the most frigid temperatures. Day by day, Mrs. Allen added to the stock until there was enough to serve the 300 guests who usually attended her New Year's Day party.

New Year's Day social observances in Morristown at the turn of the century followed a set pattern. The initial stop for "Happy New Year" wishes was a scrambled egg brunch with such mouth-watering side dishes as deerfoot sausage and thinly sliced Virginia ham and bacon at the Grinnell Willis mansion on South Street from 11:30 a.m. to 1:30 p.m. Next, the 400 proceeded to the Ridley Watts mansion on Madison Avenue for early afternoon refreshments: claret and sauterne punch for the ladies, the bar for the men. Third call was the Allen's, then on to the Charles Bradley mansion, also on Canfield Road, where society lingered until close to 6 p.m. when they went to the Seth Thomas "Red Gate Farm" for a banquet. Every year it featured something different and exotic in the way of food.

In 1924, one Morristown estate, "Cherrycroft," achieved notoriety when a local newspaper headlined the news that E.V. Brewster, a millionaire publisher, had acquired the estate for a reported $250,000 from Dudley Olcott II as a "love nest" for Miss Corliss Palmer, a southern beauty.

Brewster, the publisher of a chain of movie magazines, met Miss Palmer when she won a beauty contest sponsored by his magazines. He eventually married her in 1926 after his wife sued for divorce.

Of all the mansions built in Morristown, the mansion of Theodore N. Vail, first president of the American Telephone and Telegraph Company, is perhaps the most impressive. Located on South Street, the marble and granite mansion, completed in 1917, was never occupied by Vail, who died in 1920. When no group or society stepped forward to operate it as a museum, as he wished, it was deeded to the town by his adopted daughter and served as the municipal building for 74 years.

One of its most impressive details are the bronze doors that depict highlights of the history of Morristown in eight separate panels. They show Washington's headquarters; Washington receiving communion at Morristown; Alexander Graham Bell in conference with Professor Joseph Henry seeking advice on development of the telephone; Alfred Vail's father and mother taking their meal between services in the churchyard of the First Presbyterian Church in Parsippany; Lieutenant Colonel Alexander Hamilton courting Betsy Schuyler while he was Washington's aide; General Washington and his wife Martha watching the skirmish at Springfield in June 1780; and Alfred Vail and Samuel F.B. Morse working on the telegraph.

It was an era in which scandal rated only second to the exploitation of the masses. Divorce was not uncommon among the wealthy. Showgirls used to race around the Morristown Green in horse-drawn carriages driven by Eugene Higgins. One millionaire admitted to acquiring a yacht on which to entertain his girlfriends. Others frequented a bordello in the center of Morristown. Newspaper headlines and society gossip columns screamed the news of the indiscretions of the elite.

The names of many of the most influential families of the Gilded Age are to be found everywhere today in our culture and in the advancement from the Industrial Revolution into the twentieth century. Otto H. Kahn, a Jew whose nationality created more controversy in social Morristown than any other non-political figure of his day, twice saved a sick and dying Metropolitan Opera with his generosity and management skills; Twombly was one of the three early backers of Thomas Edison's experiments to develop the electric light bulb; the marble and granite mansion Theodore N. Vail built on South Street was donated to Morristown for a municipal building; Mrs. George W. Jenkins endowed a chair of medicine at New York University for $100,000 only several months after she and her nephew Marcellus Hartley Dodge had given $500,000 to Columbia University, his alma mater, for the erection of dormitories; and Mrs. Dodge built Madison, the finest municipal building in the nation for a town its size. Her gift had one stipulation. The Democratic candidate for mayor had to be defeated in the November elections. He was.

Their gifts of both talent and dollars, if and when they became known, were outstanding. A few, especially in the "Roaring 20s," sought the publicity a gift brought. Others, like Otto H. Kahn, shunned publicity.

Their legacy today in some degree or measure touches almost every segment of our lives through their local philanthropy made possible by trusts, gifts, and donations, both while they were alive and since. Some donations involved money, others deeds. Many were made anonymously.

Grinnell Willis, a capitalist and importer, was one of Morristown's greatest philanthropists. He built the Morristown–Morris Township Library, initially a symmetrical stone structure of English medieval style with a square tower and leaded glass (1917), donated thousands of dollars to the Morristown School starting in 1910, and was one of two men who financed conversion of the fire-gutted ruins of the Library Lyceum into an armory.

George T. Cobb, iron merchant, congressman, state senator, and Morristown's first mayor, donated the land and $100,000 to build the Methodist Church (1870), land and money to build Morristown's first public school (1869), and land for Evergreen Cemetery; Miss Ella Mabel Clark, daughter of Charles Finny Clark, president of New York's Bradstreet Company, a bronze life-size statue of George Washington astride his horse (1928); W. Parson Todd, Morristown mayor and president of a copper mining firm, a Spanish-American War statue and creation of Macculloch Hall as a museum; George G. Kip, a millionaire New York lawyer, the first unit of Morristown Memorial Hospital as a memorial to his wife (1898); Peter H.B. Frelinghuysen, the Havermeyer Contagious unit of Memorial Hospital (1917); D. Willis James, Madison's library and a large building containing an opera house, assembly room, offices, and stores to support it, a park, funds to renovate The Green, and a granite fountain to provide water for horses; and Miss Marguerite Keasbey, the Keasbey Memorial Foundation to finance the education of English children after World War II with a gift of £357,000.

*The white marble and granite mansion of Theodore N. Vail, first president of the American Telephone and Telegraph Company, went under construction in South Street in 1916. After his death in 1920, when no one would operate it as a museum, his heirs gave it to the town for a municipal building.*

Some millionaires left their estates to Morris County. Typical was Matilda Frelinghuysen, who gave her estate, "Whippany Farms," to the Morris County Park Commission for development as an arboretum named in memory of her father, George Griswold Frelinghuysen. There were also Mrs. Paul Moore, who gave the park commission the racetrack at the end of South Street for development as a riding academy; and Miss Caroline Foster, who left her farm, "Fosterfields," to the park commission for development as New Jersey's first living farm.

While the great estates and the millionaires who occupied them were a blueprint through the 1920s for the great American dream, a fascinating story of money and influence passed on from one generation to the next, the end of an era that telescoped 40 of the most powerful years in the shaping of the United States was in sight.

The demise of the Gilded Age was brought on by the stock market crash of 1929 when, almost overnight, the nation's securities and stocks lost millions of dollars. It brought to a tragic end the long season of fable in America.

The Gilded Age's memorial service came in 1975 with the death of the last of the great dowagers of an all-but deceased society, Ethel Geraldine Rockefeller Dodge, the favorite niece of John D. Rockefeller and wife of Marcellus Hartley Dodge, the president and owner of the Remington Arms Company. She left an estate valued at $101 million.

Faced with high tax bills, losses incurred in the Depression, skyrocketing maintenance costs, and a dwindling reservoir of good, inexpensive help, the wealthy began to raze their mansions in and around Morristown, one after another. By the mid-1930s, almost half of the great homes lining The Great White Way were down and the end was nowhere in sight.

Today, only a handful of the great mansions of the Gilded Age survive in the greater Morristown area. And the number is growing smaller each year. Most, their acreage whittled by subdivisions, have become museums, churches, office buildings, colleges, private schools, clubs, county parks, arboretums, private residences, and sites for condominium developments.

# 6. Clubs Founded by and for the Wealthy

The Morris County Golf Club was the only one of its kind in the world in 1894. It was founded by and for women. Gentlemen, much to their amazement and amusement, were allowed only "associate memberships" in what was to become a center for the swagger set after the clubhouse was built and the links laid out on Madison Avenue. Society leaders such as Mrs. Hamilton McKown Twombly, Miss Nina Howland, Mrs. Louis Thebaud, Mrs. Charles Scribner, Mrs. George Frelinghuysen, Mrs. Rudolph Kissel, Mrs. Richard A. McCurdy, and Mrs. Gustav Kissel got the ball rolling on April 10, 1894 at a meeting at the mansion of Mrs. Harry Hopkins.

By the date of the initial tournament, September 3, 1894, the regular membership was 32, all ladies. An additional 200 ladies were permitted "limited membership" and 200 gentlemen, associate membership.

The only man to get into the act was John D. Canfield, who leased the women the 60-acre tract for the club for a five-year period with an option of purchase. All of the club's officers and executive committee members were women, basically the grande dames of Morristown society.

Miss Nina (Cornelia) Howland, the reigning golden-haired belle of the Newport season in 1871, was the initial president. Mrs. Twombly was vice president; Mrs. William Shippen, recording secretary; Miss Alice Field, corresponding secretary; and Mrs. Charles Bradley, treasurer.

New members received notice of their election, following application, from the executive committee on the club's brilliant blue embossed stationery:

> We take pleasure in informing you that at a meeting of the executive committee of the Morris County Golf Club you were elected a member of the club, and trust our action will prove agreeable to you. The initiation fee is five dollars, and the annual dues $10 payable before June 1st.

This brief notice in 1894 carried the printed signatures of Gertrude Thebaud, Anna F. Tilden, Sara L.B. Frelinghuysen, Ina M. Kissel, and Fanny L. Hopkins. A

*The punch bowl of the Morris County Golf Club is shown here. Golfers are on its lip. Sheep, used to keep the grass short, are at the bottom. Now filled in, it is the site of an office building.*

footnote in tiny print added that "checks to the order of the Morris County Golf Club may be sent to Mrs. Marmaduke Tilden, Madison, N.J."

The landscape at the new club, which was squeezed between Madison Avenue and the Delaware, Lackawanna & Western Railroad tracks, was better adapted to golfing than that at any other existing club in the country, according to an article appearing in the New London, Connecticut *Morning Telegraph*. To make it more challenging yet, ditches and stone walls were added as extra hazards.

The picturesque 70- by 32-foot Colonial-style clubhouse, designed by Robert C. Walsh, Morristown architect, contained two large rooms extending two stories in height, with balconies around the first floor, an immense fireplace and great chimney, paneled walls, 70-foot verandas, and dressing rooms. It burned in 1903. Nearby was the carriage house and the headquarters of the golf master James Campbell, a Scot noted for his knowledge of the game.

Golf as a sport, whether played by men in plus fours or women in long skirts, was not entirely new to Morris County. At the time, Robert D. Foote, Otto H. Kahn, Charles W. McAlpin, and Alfred B. Whitney, all residents of the greater Morristown area, had practice courses on their estates.

As the club expanded, the ladies agreed that the one-and-one-third-mile-long course, which sported holes with such imaginative names as The Ideal; The Devil's Punchbowl; The Hoodoo, which crossed the railroad tracks; The Blasted Hopes; and the Setting Sun, should be expanded to 18 holes.

The men concurred, ruffling the club's and their wives' and daughters' leadership with their insistence that the club be incorporated, the land purchase option accepted, and the men elevated to positions of control.

A meeting was held by the men in January 1895 and when it was over, Paul Revere headed a slate of gentlemen officers as president of the Morris County Golf Club. How this was achieved can only be imagined. There is no public record.

It was then Revere's task to inform Miss Howland, who was not at the meeting, of the change in command and to offer her the position of honorary president. Animated with courage, Revere called formally at her estate, "Maple Cottage" on James Street. It was a long session. He never repeated exactly what was said. But he returned home pale, shaken, and mopping his brow.

"Never do I expect to put in such an afternoon again," he told his family. Miss Howland refused the honorary office, which then went to Mrs. Marmaduke Tilden, and Howland seldom entered the clubhouse again.

Before the year was out, the club was incorporated, elected an associate member of the United States Golf Association, and the initial steps taken to purchase 98 acres of property for slightly less than $70,000.

For years, the golf club was more than just a place for the wealthy to meet on common grounds to participate in sports. In less than two decades (1894–1914), it became a center of a country society. Here were held sumptuous costume balls, informal dances, beef steak dinners, receptions, weddings, private dinners, and United States Golf Association national tournaments that attracted the leaders of society and golfers from throughout the nation.

Typical was a headline in the *Newark News* of November 1, 1900: "Brilliant Society Event at Morristown, Dinner Dance Given at the Golf Club Largely Attended by Wealth and Beauty." The account described the event as a "picturesque affair, the splendors of which surpassed anything ever attempted before in the social line."

Miss Mary S. Whitney won the initial tournament held at the club, the landscape of which in three months had changed from rough grading to smooth lawns dotted with flower beds. The ladies teed off in the morning, arriving in natty golf costumes followed by their caddies shouldering the bags of golf clubs. The men began to play at 3 p.m. A few were in regulation golf costumes that ran the gamut of imagination from Scotch garters to tweed hats. A good many wore their tennis clothes, and a few came in unconventional makeup that caused some to liken the members of the club to New Jersey farmers. W. Alstone Flagg was the men's champion.

The tournament was mainly to pick the best players to defend the club's cup in October at the first woman's golf tournament in this country. Three years later, the club was the site of the United States Golf Association Women's Championship.

The two-handled solid silver challenge cups, awarded at the first inter-club tournament, were designed by Tiffany and Company. One prize was for the ladies; the other for the men. The ladies' cup was the gift of club president Nina

Howland; the men's, the gift of Mrs. Hamilton McKown Twombly. Upon the front of each were etched golfers.

Descriptions of early golfing attire were vivid and descriptive. One account stated:

> The women were usually attired in short dresses coming to about the tops of their shoes, enabling the walker to get over the grounds with its numerous rough places and hazards with ease and dexterity. Included were bright red waists and deep brown skirts, supplemented by a red and brown golf cape. The male golfer is a thing of weird and mysterious beauty. His stockings are Scotch plaid and combine more colors than were in St. Joseph's coat. His trousers bear a close resemblance to the divided skirt. He wears usually a white sweater and a "Tam O' Shanter" hat.

Many of these early golf costumes and scenes at the Morris County Golf Club have been preserved in the paintings of A.B. Frost, a club member and Morristown artist. Several score of his scenes hang in the present-day clubhouse. All are collector's items.

Tragedy struck on November 8, 1903, when fire leveled the clubhouse within 45 minutes. It was replaced by a much larger clubhouse erected at a cost of $75,000. This in turn burned in September 1915, while a formal dance was in progress.

When the second clubhouse burned, the club rented "Hedgecourt," the mansion of Max Eberhardt Schmidt, opposite the golf club on Madison Avenue for $5,500, pending enlargement of the golf course and construction of the present clubhouse in 1922.

The Morris County Golf Club was perhaps the most successful of the exclusive clubs formed by the wealthy for entertainment, recreation, and play. Other clubs included the Whippany River Club, formed by 12 millionaires at a secret meeting on Wall Street, the select Morristown Club for men only, the not so stuffy Morristown Field Club, and the Essex Hunt Club.

The common people were astonished by the incessant torrent of sporting and social events with their inestimable price tags: day-long tournaments and night-long balls attended by hundreds of blue bloods. Today, only the Morristown Club, the Morristown Field Club, and the Morris County Golf Club, greatly enlarged and its clubhouse moved to a new location, survive.

The golf club and the Whippany River Club were the most elite, seldom admitting to membership those not in the 400.

## THE WHIPPANY RIVER CLUB

The Whippany River Club was organized December 10, 1903 at a quiet meeting at 35 Wall Street in New York. Present were such Morristown personages as Robert McCurdy, R.H. Williams, Rudolph Kissel, Gordon McDonald, Benjamin Nicoll, Robert D. Foote, Norman Henderson, Arthur R. Whitney, Frederick O. Spedden, W. DeLancy Kountze, Francis H. Kinnicutt, and Louis Thebaud.

*Dressed in the golf costume of the day, a man drives off a crude tee before the turn of the century at the Morris County Golf Club. Nine holes were squeezed between Madison Avenue and the Delaware, Lackawanna & Western Railroad tracks. Nine others were located across the tracks.*

Their combined wealth exceeded $68 million and that of the charter members, $250 million. Yet this famous club never had enough money. In fact, in some years, the treasury went into the red by as much as $2,700. At such times, members dug down into their well-padded pockets and came forth with loans, which were later repaid without interest.

Members included the presidents of large firms, railroad executives, financial tycoons, and such glittering sportsmen as Alfred Vanderbilt, C. Ledyard Blair of Bernardsville, Henry Munn of Orange, and Adolph de Bary of Summit.

Benjamin Nicoll, noted Morristown polo player and head of the iron, steel, and coal firm of B. Nicoll and Company, was elected president by the initial board of governors January 22, 1904; Charles Cutler, a telephone magnate, vice president; Norman Henderson, secretary; and F.O. Spedden, treasurer. All were Morristown area residents.

Almost immediately, members leased the vast estate of Eugene Higgins with its mansion, racetrack, polo fields, sports complex, stables, and carriage house. They then made arrangements for the Delaware, Lackawanna & Western Railroad to stop at a small station they built near the main gate, and set the date for the first polo match on June 11, 1904.

Within one year, members approved issuance of $100,000 in stock and the purchase of the property for $60,000, neither of which ever occurred. Instead, the club, beriddled by monetary problems, reduced the purchase ante to $50,000 and annually renewed the lease for $1,500.

In 1910, the clubhouse, the former Higgins mansion, was destroyed by fire, prompting the board of governors to explore the consequences of throwing in the towel. The club's first president, Benjamin Nicoll, was appointed a committee of one to consult with Ransom H. Thomas, the fifth president of the Morris County Golf Club, on the possibility of combining the two socially prominent clubs and constructing a polo field on the golf course property.

On February 3, 1911, Nicoll reported the results of his conference with Thomas. It was not favorable. The Whippany River Club, if such a consolidation took place, would be expected to raise the greater portion of the $40,000 considered necessary to erect stables and construct a polo field.

The idea of consolidation died, but not the spending, a great portion of it financed by loans from club members to recuperate from the fire that had forced closing of the clubhouse, the discharging of all help, selling of all supplies, and the cancelling of the lease.

In rapid succession, a cottage with a wide veranda was renovated as a clubhouse, dressing rooms with lockers constructed, showers installed, and a 20-year lease authorized. Hunts were instituted, and discussions held on plans for laying out a golf course on the grounds. The fire that destroyed the clubhouse was described as the "worst and biggest in Morristown in 1910." Damage was estimated at more than $30,000.

*The clubhouse of the Whippany River Club, on the Eugene Higgins Estate in Morris Township, burned in 1910. Though the combined wealth of its members exceeded $250 million, the club never seemed to have enough money, forcing members to dig in their pockets.*

By the time the fire department arrived, all the buildings, which were in a connected group, were a mass of flames shooting in all directions. The blaze started in the roof over the ballroom, spread to the kitchen and the sitting room, then to the enclosed riding academy, known as Tan Court, and the squash court, a $10,000 structure built the previous year.

It was at the club that the legions of the 400 gathered for parties, sports, and entertainment, both good and wicked. They came to participate in and view sporting events, exercise, trap shoot, dance, play polo, tennis, handball, and squash, and to learn to ride horseback. Here were held dog shows, concerts, hunt breakfasts, horse races, fireworks displays, tennis tournaments, flower shows, wedding receptions, and parties.

These men of wealth and position, many with a taste for gambling, did not lack the facilities nor the opportunities, both among themselves and with outside professional bookies, to place bets. The bookmakers, most of them from New York, swarmed into Morristown during the races at the Whippany River Club, ready to cover any bet offered. Eventually, they became a nuisance and the object of sermons by ministers of the town, actions that prompted their being shooed away from the track by police. But the action did not end the betting. It still went on among the wealthy members. One heavy bettor, who later married a niece of Andrew Carnegie, is said to have lost thousands of dollars betting on the horses at the races.

Some members did more than merely pay the $50-per-year dues. Messers. Nicoll, Otto H. Kahn, and Dr. Leslie Ward in 1910 contributed $500 for the construction of a shooting park, R.H. Williams six years later presented the club with a gift of $1,000, and Samuel H. Gillespie, foregoing money, gave the club 50 sheep to keep the grass short.

Trap shooting became a major sport at the new shooting park. A team of crack shots fielded by the club won competition after competition in North Jersey. No less than five shooting trophies were awarded by the club in 1917. Included was the President's Trophy, donated by Edward P. Meany; the Freeman Trophy, donated by S. Harold Freeman; the Ross Trophy, donated by Leland H. Ross; the Olcott Trophy, donated by Dudley Olcott; and the Henry Cup, donated by George G. Henry.

In 1905, an attempt was made to provide transportation between the club and the mansions of those Mendham and Bernardsville men who were members. The Magnet, a road coach drawn by four horses, ran regularly in the spring and summer between the club and Bernardsville via Mendham, leaving at 4 p.m. each afternoon.

Polo matches drew large crowds of spectators. An advertisement of the day notes two matches between the Rumson Country Club and the Whippany River Club on October 3 and October 6. Admission to the grandstands was $1. Parking space was free.

## THE MORRISTOWN CLUB—FOR MEN ONLY

Two non-members in 1903 succeeded where the fairer sex had failed, except on New Year's Day. Engineer Benjamin Day and conductor David Sanderson, two of the best known trainmen on the Delaware, Lackawanna & Western Railroad's Millionaires Express were invited to a gathering at the exclusive Morristown Club, a haven for men only. In the billiard room, the two men, still in work clothes, were presented gold watches, the backs of which were monogrammed and the inside of the lids inscribed with a tribute to their "fidelity and unvarying courtesy." In addition, each received $80 in gold.

Twin testimonials on parchment signed by the grateful commuters were presented to the trainmen. Signatures included those of Richard McCurdy, John Waterbury, Albert Vernam, Hamilton McKown Twombly, Ransom Thomas, Alexander Tiers, and George G. Kip. Seven years later, the same signatories gathered once again to honor Sanderson, this time to attend his funeral.

The Morristown Club, founded in 1884 by 12 captains of industry, was not incorporated until 1887. It had both dignity and decorum despite its early name changes and many different quarters. The bar and card room were big favorites. There was a pool, a squash court from 1887 to 1914, a billiard room in 1901, and ping pong in 1902. For a time in 1887, a country headquarters in Morris Plains sported two grass tennis courts, a bowling alley, and a pigeon shoot.

In its infancy, the club met in the library and Lyceum, calling itself first the Morristown Club, then the Morristown Casino, and finally reverting to its original name.

Members first rented a too-large house at Maple Avenue and Boyken Street (now Miller Road), but the rent was too high for the $25 initiation fee and $25 annual dues. So the club made the first of many moves to 54 South Street before purchasing its present home at 27 Elm Street in 1919.

The Morristown Club, with its distinctive rooms, values, and rituals, reflected a place of bliss for many of its members. For some it was a way-station en route home from the canyons of New York; for others a place for a friendly game of cards, a chat, a chance to catch up on reading, or a cocktail.

One was likely to meet bank presidents, stockbrokers, lawyers, mercantile princes, former governors, legislators, musicians, authors, financiers, and tycoons. Many were noted yachtsmen, members of trap shooting and polo teams, golfers, and scholars.

To them, the Morristown Club was a home away from home with comfortable leather chairs, a bar, a newspaper room with a club servant to quickly repair the symptoms of disarray, and hearty menus featuring mutton chops, stuffed boiled kidney, and steaks.

House rules were explicit. Crackers and cheese were to be served in the pool room only (1890), drinks were not to be served in the front room on Sunday until after the shades were drawn, and no horse or vehicle could stand in front of the clubhouse for more than five minutes between 11:55 p.m. on Saturday and 9 a.m. on Monday.

Rooms for gentlemen desiring to stay overnight, a week, or a month were simple in furnishings and price. The tab for bedrooms in 1890 was fixed at $1.50 per day, $7 a week, or $25 a month.

The step that threatened to reduce the entire operation to chaos came in 1887 when the board of governors voted to allow families and ladies the privileges of "Brookbank," the cottage of Arthur Thompson at Morris Plains, known as the club's country house. The action was quickly repealed, as rapidly in fact as the board could be reconvened. For a time, ladies were guests one day a year only: New Year's Day. In recent years, however, they have been allowed on more occasions.

Early presidents of the club included such names as Frederick Wood; George S. Wylie, in whose administration the action to open the country house to families was taken, then quickly repealed; Joseph Bushnell; Albert H. Vernam; and George G. Kip.

## THE MORRISTOWN FIELD CLUB

The picture of a debutante woman attired in colorful hunt club regalia astride a black horse was posted throughout Morristown in the fall of 1910. It announced the annual Field Club Horse Show October 6, 7, and 8.

The event, a major society occurrence, was usually preceded by the annual Horse Show Dance and Dinner, both held at the Morris County Golf Club; numerous private parties, both at the club and at different estates; and teas and socials.

Typical was the round of dinner parties scheduled for 1910. Dr. and Mrs. Granville M. White entertained 40 guests; Mr. and Mrs. Dudley Olcott, 16 guests;

*House rules at the exclusive Morristown Club, a gathering place for men only on Elm Street, were explicit. Crackers and cheese were to be served in the pool room only, drinks were not to be served in the front room on Sunday until the shades were drawn, and no card games could be played on Sunday.*

*Judging four-in-hands at the Morristown Field Club's annual horse show, started in 1897 at the club grounds in South Street. Four categories were judged: roadsters, harness horses, saddle horses, and hunters and jumpers.*

Mr. and Mrs. Robert D. Foote, 8 guests; Mr. and Mrs. Peter H.B. Frelinghuysen, 10 guests; Harry Hoyt, 4 guests; and John Mayer Jr., 6 guests.

The Horse Show Dinner itself was attended by the 10 members of the committee and the exhibitors. It usually preceded by one night the dance, a gala affair that drew exhibitors from the local estates and as far afield as the Virginia countryside and New England. Attendance was by invitation only.

An early newspaper account termed the horse shows, held at the clubhouse grounds on South Street, "equal to any exhibitions in the country with one exception, the New York Horse Show in Madison Square Garden." For society, attendance was a must.

The shows were bright with the jingle of harness bells and the sheen of million-dollar horse flesh. Some of the animals were fresh from tracks and exhibitions at Saratoga and Long Island. Private boxes were sold at auction for a handsome fee, but many of the spectators lined up along the rail; others vied for space behind it to park a carriage from which to view the show.

There would be Judge Moore, noted breeder of hackney stock; Otto H. Kahn showing his favorite horses, Starlight and Golight in tandem, or his pair of harness horses Impetus and Icarus; Walter Bliss with Lady Whitefoot and Lady Lightfoot; and Mrs. Paul Moore with her Kara drawing a ladies' basket phaeton. There were classes for ponies, hunters, jumpers, saddle horses, road horses, fire horses, and in later years, officer's mounts.

But most exciting were the four-in-hands. The Hamilton McKown Twombly's showed theirs. So did Otto H. Kahn and Bexley Holcombe, a self-made

112

millionaire in oil with bristling gray mustache and gray topper who competed in coach-and-four races in London and on the continent on visits abroad.

The Field Club was founded in the spring of 1881 by a group of women as the Morristown Lawn Tennis Club, using grass courts on the property of William B. Skidmore (now Peck School). With the erection of his opulent mansion, the club moved two blocks west to the Lidgerwood estate (now the site of Kings supermarket) and expanded its athletic billing to include baseball, softball, football, touch football, cricket, golf, bowling, croquet, ping pong, figure skating, hockey, field hockey, shooting, and squash.

Members went in big for tennis tournaments, set off fireworks on the Fourth of July, gave elaborate social functions to which notables in the sporting world of the day were invited, and sponsored varied teams.

In spite of an active membership of 450 in 1904, the club was never run on more than a shoestring financially. It built its own clubhouse (destroyed by fire in 1917) in 1894 at a cost of $2,500. It was one story in height with wide piazzas on three sides. Included was a large room exclusively for the ladies, one for the gentlemen, and a large meeting room between the two.

It did not come into its own as the Morristown Field Club, however, until 1910 when its name was changed from the Lawn Tennis Club. Evidence of the social standing of the Field Club, despite the fact that almost anyone could join that was athletically inclined, is seen by its listing in the *Morristown Society Directory*. Not only were its officers named year after year, but also the various club committees.

From 1905 to 1916, during the club's heyday as a tennis mecca, all of the New Jersey State Tennis Tournaments were played on its courts, two of which were located on what today is the sidewalk in front of Kings Supermarket on South Street. Many of these state tournaments were won by club members, including such names as Miss Alice Day in 1907; Karl Behr, a nationally ranked Field Club member; and Edward P. Larden, seeded number one in the United States.

Exhibition matches were a big thing, drawing the cream of society as spectators. Players included such big-time names as Bill Tilden, United States men's singles champion from 1920 to 1925, the first American to win England's Wimbledon Championship, and the leader of the United States team that won the Davis Cup from 1920 to 1926.

In 1910, Miss Alice Leslie Hill, one of the last of the grande dames of Morristown's Old Guard, won the ladies singles championship at the Field Club. She savored the memory of her victory throughout her lifetime. When her household effects were auctioned off, the silver trophy dish awarded her went for a few dollars.

# 7. Into the Twentieth Century

They've called it "a treasure," "one of the most historic spots in the eastern United States," " Morristown's most prized possession," "The town's most distinguishing feature," "Morristown's jewel," and "the common possession of every citizen of Morristown."

It has been bought, sold, given away, divided into two sections by a road, fenced in as a pasture, used as a parade ground, and coveted by merchants and real estate speculators for two centuries.

But, if you're a native of Morristown, it's The Green, a 2.5-acre park surrounded by many of the town's main businesses and stores and circled by Route 24. To newcomers or out-of-towners, The Green, rich in historic lore, may be "The Park," "The Square," or the "Center."

Over the years, its been the scene of hangings, the site of the first Morristown schoolhouse and county courthouse, a Christmas wonderland, a gathering place for "hippies," a paradise for pigeons, the setting for civic celebrations and community festivals, and a place for just strolling or sitting.

Only the surroundings have changed since 1908 when John R. Brinley, a local landscape architect, divided the square Green into eight triangles by walks and flower beds. The project was underwritten by Daniel Willis James, Madison philanthropist, a partner and the senior member of Phelp's Dodge Company, and a man worth $25 million.

Earlier, in 1878, Frederick Law Olmstead, the man who designed New York's Central Park, met with the Board of Aldermen to discuss improving The Green, which officials admitted was badly in need of renovation. No action was taken, however, on Olmstead's suggestions.

Over the years, it has been ornamented with sundry objects ranging from monuments, bronze tablets, a liberty pole, the town flag pole, a small schoolhouse, the county courthouse and jail, Civil War cannon, the town well and pump, the 5-foot-tall whipping post, the pillory and stocks, and on occasion, the gallows.

Aldermanic candidates have campaigned for office on it, distributing literature and giving political speeches. As early as 1971, arts and crafts festivals were held there. At Christmas, it is the site of Santa Land.

*This image is a view of The Green shortly after the turn of the century. The walkways remain the same today. Traffic in Park Place was not regulated and went in both directions.*

In the 1960s, there were anti-war demonstrations protesting the United States's involvement in the war in Vietnam. A decade later, crowds of young people, called "hippies" by many of the townspeople, took over The Green's lawns and benches, to sit and talk, play guitars, read, and picnic.

After the installation of lights and increased police patrols, The Green again began to attract its more usual patronage: senior citizens, who clustered there to chat and feed the pigeons; mothers with baby strollers; and office workers, who purchased hot dogs and soda from curbside vendors during their lunch breaks.

Most of the young people were "good kids," one policeman said, not involved in vandalism or narcotics. It was only a few, he added, who caused trouble.

The transformation from a youth-dominated drug haven to an outdoor cafeteria can be traced to two major developments of the early 1980s: the construction of Headquarters Plaza office towers, hotel, and mall, and the 1981 renovation of The Green.

Its deterioration over the years was evident even to the most casual observer. There were broken curbs, crumbling walkways, broken benches, vast stretches of bare ground, sparse, tired looking shrubs struggling for survival, and dead or dying trees. Even the iron fence that surrounded the Civil War monument, badly damaged by vandals, was gone.

The movement to renovate The Green started in 1979 when the Morristown Rotary Club chose restoration of The Green as its 75th anniversary project. The club's action was followed by the formation of Morristown Beautiful, Inc., a committee dedicated to providing a new look for The Green, which obtained $150,000 from Green Acres. The remainder of the money was raised from area corporations, merchants, professional people, civic organizations, and individuals.

Following a feasibility study, Morristown Beautiful assembled a renovation committee chaired by Ralph Cutler Jr., and engaged a landscape artist, Anna Young of Mendham. She spent 66 hours on The Green observing everything that went on from pedestrian and vehicular traffic to where park users walked.

Her recommendations were structured around the basic plan laid out by Brinley in 1908, and provided for more and new benches along walkways and streets, encouraged the use of the lawn as a passive sitting area, and provided for an additional paved area to offset one in the heavily used center of The Green. She also called for relocation and redesign of flower beds, new plantings of barberry and yew shrubs, and increased lighting.

To survey the trees, horticultural students from the Morris County Vocational Technical School spent a week studying The Green, finding 11 trees dead or dying and another three or four that needed pruning and fertilization.

An archeological study of The Green by students from Drew University in Madison unearthed 1,800 artifacts from 54 3.5-foot-deep, 8-inch holes bored in The Green's 2.5 acres. Their most significant discoveries were a brick walk that once traversed The Green diagonally; a gully near the Methodist Church where children were believed to have swum; pieces of porcelain dishes from Holland; a public well south of North Park Place; a cellar hole filled with trash, which may

*Carriages pause beside The Green on West Park Place in 1910. The building in the background was known as "drug store corner."*

have been Morristown's first landfill; and a glass globe from a lamp of a trolley that once ran around The Green.

Today, parking meters have replaced the wooden hitching posts once located every few feet around The Green to tie horses and buggies to; one way traffic, effective in 1926, has replaced what some called "the nightmare" of two way traffic; and cars no longer park head-on to the curb.

The Green attracts its largest crowds of youngsters and adults during the Christmas season, when Santa presides in his Yule house in the center of The Green's Santa Land, asking each and every youngster their wish for Christmas morning.

For the first time since 1873, Santa Claus returned to The Green in 1948. He landed his sleigh atop the Park Square Building, descended a ladder to a fire truck, and took up residence in a little house on The Green built by John Ginty, former mayor of Morris Township. The furnishings for the house were made by Morristown High School students.

In 1968, however, Christmas on The Green fell on hard times. The breathtaking displays had fallen into disrepair: gone were the giant rocking horses, oversize story books, and figures of Frosty the Snowman and Fred Flintstone. Breakage had resulted in fewer light displays and decorations. But, saddest of all was the fact that Santa had no house. The Victorian house, centerpiece of the Thomas Nast Christmas Village, had been declared unsafe and there were insufficient funds to repair it. A new house had been ordered, but would not be ready until the following year.

Some folks blamed the merchants who failed to adequately fund Christmas on The Green. But the Christmas on The Green committee pointed out there were fewer merchants to donate as mom and pop stores and small shops disappeared. Records show that only three of the thirty merchants located directly on The Green donated to the Christmas display.

By 1988, the number of Christmas decorations adorning The Green had shrunk to one-half of what they were in 1986. Officials blamed it on lack of storage space, lack of funds, and lingering debts. Usually, the contributions from merchants ranged between $4,000 and $6,000. In 1988, the amount contributed was $700. A total of 1,000 flyers mailed to potential private donors garnered $175 compared to $2,500 in previous years. Yet, despite the reduced decorations, 7,000 to 8,000 people attended the annual Christmas parade.

In the past several years, Baby Jesus was stolen from the Creche; one of two rocking horses, a favorite of children, was destroyed on Christmas Eve, 1992; and one of the Wise Men was defaced with spray paint in 1989.

In 1993, a story in the *Newark Star Ledger* related the increased vandalism. Its headline read: "Vandalism on Green. Trashing of Christmas Display Becomes Ugly Holiday Ritual."

A 25-year maintenance agreement between the Trustees of The Green and the town set rigid guidelines for the upkeep of The Green, ranging from the genus and species of bushes to be planted to the allowable height of the grass.

The agreement requires the town to pay the maintenance costs, which run about $45,000 annually, and requires an outside landscape contractor rather than public work crews to do the work.

The latest addition to The Green is a $500,000 life-size statue and fountain at the main South Park Place entrance to The Green erected in 2001. It depicts a minuteman, his wife clutching a baby, their son, and his dog.

## THE TROLLEY ARRIVES

With shrieking whistle drowning out the cheers of crowds that lined both sides of Speedwell Avenue, many waving handkerchiefs, Morristown's first trolley car rumbled down the street under its own current, stopping in front of the municipal building on August 22, 1909.

In the 40-passenger car were town officials and citizens who rode from Morris Plains at the invitation of the Morris County Traction Company, the operator of the trolley line. As the passengers alighted from the trolley to have their picture taken standing in front of the car, eager children of all ages climbed aboard for a free ride.

Many called the arrival of the trolley in its bright new colors of green and yellow the real beginning of modern Morristown's business district, terming it a vehicle that could provide inexpensive transportation to the town's shopping center for farmers and out of town residents, many of whom previously relied on a horse and buggy.

To power the trolley, the traction company leased a vacant lot on Speedwell Avenue, across from Speedwell Place, on which it placed a roofed-over flatcar installing in it an 120-kilowatt generator that generated 2,300 volts of alternating current. Later current was provided by the Morris and Somerset Electric Company.

For its inaugural run, the trolley had been brought on the Delaware, Lackawanna & Western Railroad to Morris Plains from Dover where it was placed on the newly installed tracks.

Eventually, the trolley ran around The Green and west as far as Lake Hopatcong and east down Morris Street to Springfield. In 1920, the company began sponsoring moonlight excursions from Morristown to Lake Hopatcong. They advertised: "Rarely could so much romance be purchased for $1," the cost of a round trip trolley ride plus a boat trip on the lake.

When the trolley tracks ran around The Green in East, West, North and South Park Place in 1911, the street around The Green was dirty and bumpy with traffic going two ways. When it was paved, Park and Telford blocks (similar to Belgium blocks) were laid as a foundation.

At its peak in 1920, three years before the company went into receivership, the trolley transported 7.7 million riders a total of 1.4 million miles. The victim of small buses that stole away many passengers, the line was finally sold at public auction on the steps of the Morris County Courthouse in 1927.

The small buses, called jitneys, would often run several minutes ahead of the trolley, picking up waiting passengers, an action that infuriated the trolley drivers.

The high cost of roadbed construction and repairs to the overhead trolley lines were two of the reasons that sent the company into the hands of receivers in 1923, and the chief cause for the change to buses.

From the turn of the century to after World War I, the trolley was the most reliable and convenient form of transportation. The trolleys were fast and relatively weatherproof, especially compared to cars, which were temperamental and floundered in rain storms when dirt roads were turned into impassable quagmires. In town, the trolley went as fast as traffic. Between towns, they could reach speeds of 50 miles per hour.

The trolleys were also a lot cheaper than cars, which were a luxury, more a plaything of the rich than an essential means of transportation. The trolley ran often with a heavy proportion of its riders coming from the working public. Riding in a trolley for a nickel appealed to many, especially the younger generation, as a novelty, if not a fast way of travel.

The idea for a trolley line was born in Morristown. At the initial meeting of the incorporators, Robert D. Foote, a Morristown millionaire and president of the Iron Bank, was elected president. The company was incorporated June 8, 1899. Capital stock in the amount of $250,000 in $100 shares was issued. In June 1905, the amount was increased to $3 million and a bond issue authorized.

The trolley cars were of various sizes and designs, many of them being second hand. At first they were small cars. Then came cars resembling freight cars. One lot included bodies from the Third Avenue Railroad in New York on new wheels. At the end there were a number of steel cars, each bearing the name of Edward

*Children got free rides on the first trolley into Morristown in 1909. In its peak year, 1920, the trolley transported 7.7 million riders, a total of 1.4 million miles.*

*This section of a hollowed-out cedar log was once used as a pipe to carry water into Morristown. It was unearthed when workmen were repairing Court Street near the reservoir once located where a county parking deck is today.*

K. Mills, a director of the Federal Reserve Bank of New York and trustee for the fund for the cars' purchase.

The last trolley ran February 2, 1928. Buses, for which the firm invested $500,000, were substituted to follow the general route of the trolleys. The last vestige of the trolley tracks disappeared in 1933 when those in West Park Place were covered by pavement. Five years earlier, the tracks in Speedwell Avenue had been torn up.

In 1909, in his annual message to the Board of Aldermen, the mayor recommended the purchase of the latest in firefighting equipment and the improvement of the town's roads, which he termed "a cause of humiliation to us" due to damage caused by the installation of sewers, electric conduits, and gas mains. Describing Race Street as "a muddy sink hole," he reported five carloads of trap rock had been purchased for filling in holes in the macadam in an effort to improve the roads.

## RAILROAD TRACKS ELEVATED

The following year, the mayor stressed the need for elevation of the Delaware, Lackawanna & Western Railroad tracks through town. "The need for elevation is becoming more apparent each day, he said, noting the "existing conditions are becoming more congested and in many respects are blocking the progress of the town."

120

The railroad first approached the town fathers in 1908 with the idea of elevating the tracks, moving them 100 feet north, and building a new railroad station and platforms. Work on the project progressed for several years. It involved new storm water mains, rearrangement of pipe and lines of various utilities serving the town, construction of a bridge to carry the railroad over Morris Street, movement of buildings including a firehouse, laying of new trolley tracks, and paving of Morris Street.

The elevation of the tracks eliminated all grade crossings in Morristown and prompted B.W. Clifford, chairman of the board of Aldermen Track Elevation Committee, to term the project "one that will be of lasting benefit to the town."

The track elevation project was followed in 1910 by installation of sewers and construction of a sewerage disposal treatment plant.

## MORRISTOWN'S WATER SUPPLY

Morristown's water supply has a long and unique history, first being privately owned and known as the Morris Aqueduct Company, incorporated in 1799 by 26 residents. An aqueduct 4 miles long, including its various branches, was constructed at a cost of $3,000 to a fountain 100 feet above the town on what is now Western Avenue. From there, water was conducted to town through brick tiles.

Some years the aqueduct was dry, forcing residents to depend on wells until James Wood purchased the company. He repaired the aqueduct, laying hollowed-out cedar logs, each 11 feet long, to bring water gathered in little reservoirs in the Jockey Hollow area to the fountain on what is now Western Avenue. From there, water was conducted to town through brick tile.

In 1846, John F. Voorhees acquired the aqueduct, replaced the hollowed-out cedar logs with cement and cast iron pipe, and constructed a distributing reservoir on Fort Nonsense Hill (now the site of a two-deck Morris County parking garage). When repairing Court Street in the 1970s, workmen uncovered several sections of the hollowed-out cedar logs that had served as water mains.

In 1912, before the era of water meters, the price of water to each subscriber to the system was $18 a year. Water restrictions during a drought or lack of water are not new. On August 28, 1880, the proprietors of the Morris Aqueduct Company published the following announcement in *The Jerseyman*:

> A very unusual shrinkage in the flow of our springs with an unavoidable loss of water incident to the excavation of our new reservoir has so materially shortened our supply of water that we feel compelled to stop all street and lawn sprinkling and to ask our patrons to exercise economy in the use of water for domestic purposes. The new reservoir will be done in October, but not in time to be of any use during the present dry spell.

The Morris Aqueduct Company, in 1891 and 1892, acquired land and water rights to extend their system and immediately constructed several reservoirs,

121

collecting water from numerous springs. This system was abandoned in the 1930s, seven years after Morristown purchased the company.

The *Democratic Banner,* in a story May 17, 1884, surprised everyone, especially county officials and residents of North Park Place. The story read:

> In digging the trench on North Park Place (to extend water mains) just opposite the pump near the corner of the park, workmen discovered the foundation of the old log jail, which was torn down upon completion of the present one in 1828. The foundation was found three feet below the present surface of the street. Some of the timbers of the old jail may still be seen underneath the present piazza of the United States Hotel. They are filled with wrought iron hand made nails, thickly driven in, to prevent prisoners from cutting their way through.

In 1919, Morristown voted to own and operate its own water plant. In 1931, the Clyde Potts Reservoir, designed to hold 385 million gallons of water, was built in Brookside on a 175-acre reservation. That same year, the town purchased the Normandy Water Company, its plant on Columbia Road, springs, and wells for $212,000.

## MORRISTOWN'S BEST KEPT SECRET

For almost half a century, Morristown's best kept secret, two brick-lined tunnels littered with old bottles and yellowed bills that during Prohibition connected speakeasies, a bottling plant, distillery, gambling dens, and a brothel, lay buried beneath Speedwell Avenue. Their existence came to light in 1971, 38 years after the repeal of Prohibition, when buildings lining Speedwell Avenue were being razed for a $27-million urban renewal face lifting of the business district.

One tunnel stretched the length of Speedwell Avenue, partially under the roadway, as far east as High Street. The other crossed the road and curved halfway up Clinton Street to a speakeasy and brothel.

One establishment, opposite High Street, the existence of which came to light when bulldozers moved in to raze a former firehouse, led a charmed life. It was never raided despite the efforts of two members of the Women's Christian Temperance Union who spied on it from the confines of the old Palace Theater on the opposite side of the street.

The biggest speakeasy was a night club on the second floor of the old McAlpin Building (now the site of the Century 21 Department Store) that ran wide open. There were others, much smaller in scope, in a cellar at the corner of Speedwell Avenue and Flagler Street, in a building behind the former Morey LeRue Laundry Company, at the famed Piper's Restaurant, and in a frame boarding house at Speedwell Avenue and Spring Street. Others were located in the Hollow area and in Flagler, Water, Market, and Washington Streets.

Many of the smaller speakeasies and gambling dens were operated by a group called the "Big Four," either alone or as a group. Typical was a restaurant one

*Old Morristown Reservoir on Anne Street hill was abandoned in 1926 when the Western Avenue reservoir was opened. The brick wall was demolished shortly after World War II and the area was made into a parking lot in 1949.*

Morristown resident recalls entering with a date because a trumpet player he knew played there.

"I never realized it at the time," he said "but the restaurant was a front." He added, "I suppose I should have got suspicious when I saw the owner sneak out and up the street to a nearby restaurant to get the meal we had ordered. He never cooked in the place, just served illegal whiskey and wine."

Reports vary on the size and extent of the most exclusive speakeasy opposite High Street where the elite of Morris County went to drink "the finest whiskey available." One former patron recalled, "They dug a cellar out beneath the original basement, put plumbing and furnishings in, constructed a secret stairway and the tunnels for use in the event the police ever came calling."

The entrance to the High Street speakeasy was sealed by the 1-foot-thick wall of a two-story, 10,000-gallon vat after Prohibition was repealed in 1933.

"People would not believe it today if they knew of the existence of such tunnels and the engineering design and work that went into their construction," another old-timer related. The tunnels were dug and lined during Prohibition by expert masons, one of whom worked not only in Morristown, but also in Somerville, Basking Ridge, and New York.

Much of the high grade whiskey came from Washington and Maryland. The balance, mainly applejack, wine, and bathtub gin, was manufactured in distilleries in stores and houses on Speedwell Avenue and bottled in containers manufactured next door. A curved depression in the bottom of the tunnel enabled mash to be dumped into the tunnel, which emptied into a small pond and stream behind the buildings, eventually entering the Whippany River.

"There was a regular dumping schedule," one old-timer recalled. "Heck, there had to be. Almost every other building held a speakeasy that was making illegal liquor in varying quantities. If a schedule had not been adhered to, the smell of mash would have been overpowering at the pond.

"As it was," he added, "it was often said one could get drunk by just standing on the banks of the pond and creek that carried the residue downstream."

Two large wooden vats, each 9 feet high, transported in pieces from Czechoslovakia to the United States, and 9 redwood barrels were dug up by the bulldozers. The rare oval-shaped barrels were found in the back of the winery four stories below street level. The contractor sold each of the big ones for $200 each.

The large cement wine vat was demolished and the tunnels filled in. The stores and houses that lined the east side of Speedwell Avenue too are gone. In their place has risen Headquarters Plaza with its hotel and towering glass and steel office buildings.

## THE GYPSIES
In the 1920s and 1930s, gypsy caravans used to camp during the spring and summer months in Morris Township at Lake and Lake Valley Roads at the head

*Faced by the loss of its 50,000-book library in the Lyceum fire in 1914, Grinnell Willis, noted dry goods merchant, donated funds for the construction of a large two-story fireproof library in Miller Road.*

124

of Speedwell Lake. The cry, "The gypsies are coming, here come the gypsies," echoed nearly every spring when King Naylor Harrison brought his tribe back from "wintering in the southern states." They seemed very prosperous, one newspaper account stated, with black Cadillacs to pull their shiny new chrome trailers.

When camp was pitched, the tent nearest the road belonged to the Gypsy Queen. In front of it was placed a sign representing a huge hand, palm outward, advertising that fortunes were read there.

Young men from the gypsy camp went door to door in the neighborhood selling plant stands made from white birch trees growing in the nearby woods.

*The Madison Eagle* described the arrival of the gypsies one spring:

> The fancy caravan equipment and horses were a sight to see. Brilliant trappings marked their entourage, which often consisted of as many as 35 wagons. They were not the usual nondescript and ramshackle equippages usually associated with gypsies. Rather they were brightly colored and decorated with gold leaf. They were rolling salons of beauty.

As befitted a king, Naylor Harrison rode in the most pretentious vehicle of all. His was an immense traveling home, fitted out elegantly for the maximum comfort.

In those days, $2,500 was a great deal of money, but that was the amount which King Naylor's wagon represented in cash. Each of his 11 children had a wagon and all were tended by African-American servants.

Accompanying the band would be a large drove of horses, the finest stock that King Naylor could glean in his months of search.

King Naylor, who lived on and off in Madison and Morristown for 40 years, died in 1928 at the age of 85. His funeral was held at the gypsy camp on Lake Road. Representatives from 12 states attended the services.

His wife, Mrs. Louisa Harrison, called the Queen of the Romany Gypsies, died in 1921. She left property composed of bonds, mortgages, and money equally to her children. The family by then was scattered throughout the United States and Canada. Some were with circuses and carnivals. Others were traveling traders and a few had settled permanently in various towns.

## THE MORRISTOWN–MORRIS TOWNSHIP LIBRARY

Faced with the loss of its library of 50,000 books in the Library Lyceum fire on Washington's Birthday in 1914, Grinnell Willis, noted dry goods merchant, stepped forward and donated funds for the construction of a large two-story stone fireproof library in Miller Road opposite Saint Peter's Episcopal Church. Ground for the new library was broken May 31, 1916.

The library opened its doors December 14, 1917 with 8,000 books on its shelves and a staff of four. In 1924, when the building became overcrowded with 43,500 volumes, Willis once again stepped forward, donating money to build a children's wing on the South Street side of the property.

Though a man in his 80s, Willis is remembered sitting before the fireplace in the children's wing telling stories to the children. Earlier, in 1925, he hired Samuel Yellin to design and install a magnificent wrought iron work that enhanced the beauty of the library.

The handsome golden eagle in the tower of the library was originally part of the Morristown Roll of Honor in front of the old armory building during 1917, 1918, and 1919. It was given to the library by Willis in 1920 as a memorial to those who served in World War I.

The history of the library in Morristown is traced through several associations. The first association for the circulation of books in Morristown was organized in 1792, with 97 members and 96 books. In 1812, this organization, which had grown to 123 members and 396 books, was merged into the Morristown Library Association. In 1848, a library for the benefit of the apprentices of Morris County was instituted, acquiring the collection of the Morristown Library Association. Their records show their initial 1,500 volumes soon increased to 2,500 volumes. The Morris Institute, founded in 1854, within two years was beset by poverty and fire and in 1865, its books passed to the Library Lyceum, which carried on its work for 45 years until 1914 when the building and books were destroyed by fire. At that time, a new library site was purchased at the corner of South Street and Miller Road, and the present Morristown Library, since enlarged, was erected.

## THE GREAT DEPRESSION

When the bottom fell out of Wall Street that "Black Tuesday" in October 1929, there ensued a financial panic which saw an estimated $40 billion in investment money disappear almost overnight as the Great Depression was born.

All summer long, mesmerized and confident, the country had dreamed of money and the things it could buy. There had been warnings, but they had come and gone like heat lightning. In August, the stock market had continued rising. All was well. Then came Thursday, October 24, the beginning of chaos. It was climaxed by the knockout punch on Tuesday, October 29, when stock prices fell dramatically. The resulting crash heard around the world brought to a tragic end that long fable in America. As the year wore on, the Great Depression continued to gather its momentum.

Within five days, panic gripped Wall Street and its millionaires as financial values collapsed and the gigantic structure of prosperity fell into ruins. Many of Morristown's millionaires lost millions of dollars in just hours. And the end was nowhere in sight.

As the year wore on, the Great Depression gathered its terrible momentum. Breadlines and soup kitchens appeared in the cities. Unemployment soared. An era had ended.

It started like a dull ache, one that was to last for four long, painful years. It was the day when the honeycomb of American credit collapsed to create grim chaos. A day of lost ambitions and overwhelming debts, it was a day when the fortunes of Morristown's millionaires diminished. It was little understood that autumn day that the crash would usher in grinding unemployment in Morristown, hunger, and aimlessness for four cruel years.

As time wore on, there was also fading hope, which even the relatively fortunate greater Morristown area could not escape. There were two local suicides traceable to the day. The following year, two more men committed suicide, one because of business worries and inability to find work, the other from hunger.

Indicative of the hard times and fear of what was to come was the 1929 Morris County Community Chest drive, which fell $50,000 short of its goal.

Many local investors were wiped out with huge losses when Servel Refrigerator stock, a favorite in Morristown, collapsed. One by one, people began losing jobs. While the local relief rolls grew and empty store fronts dotted the streets, Morristown, deemed somewhat affluent, survived better than the larger cities.

There were few industries in the greater Morristown area, therefore few factories to be closed. It was the small businessman who was hit the hardest during those years. He couldn't borrow money to restock his inventories, which dwindled rapidly. And most residents could not get credit for purchases.

"During the Depression, Morristown collected only 65 percent of its taxes," one Morristown official said. "But nobody foreclosed. There was nothing anybody could do. The aldermen spent whatever money they could get to help out in Morristown. Even if you only worked three days a week, that was a job. In those days, all you spent money for was food and heat."

*This view is of cars parked head-on to the curb in 1932, at the heart of the Depression and six years after one-way traffic was instituted around The Green. The Babbitt Building, Morristown's early skyscraper, is directly behind the town flag pole.*

127

*This view of Morristown is from Fort Nonsense hill in 1907. Visible is the Mill Street Public School and the steeple of the Second Presbyterian Church. During the Depression, the CCC worked in the Fort Nonsense and Jockey Hollow areas after Dutch Elm disease struck.*

"The starting of as much municipal work as possible seems to be the only prospect of relief," one official said. An ever increasing stream of eager job hunters invaded the newly opened headquarters of the Mayor's Unemployment Relief Committee in the American Legion Post building in Speedwell Avenue within weeks of the stock market crash. In one day alone, more than 75 applications for work were received.

By the dawn of 1930, the town hired 165 men who were out of work and kept them employed for four months. That Christmas, the police department distributed 200 baskets of food and during the cold winter months supported 25 families.

Building, which had been going full swing until the stock market crash, leveled off, if not dipped in the number of residences and buildings constructed. Crime increased in 1930 and 1931, especially store robberies. Police blamed the increase on economic conditions.

By early spring 1930, as stocks drifted further down, some reaching new lows, the United States Department of Labor advised municipalities to hire only local residents.

By the spring of 1931, Mayor Clyde Potts reported, "there are more people out of work this year than last, and it is up to the town to support these unfortunates."

Help-wanted ads almost disappeared from the classified sections of newspapers, replaced by advertisements for domestic auctions and furnishings for sale. The A&P sold potatoes for a penny a pound. One merchant had to sell his car to meet his payroll. Other merchants who survived, many admittedly by "the skin of their teeth," never missed a payroll, but admitted they had trouble meeting them.

By 1931, the mood in Morristown was so diffident that voting plunged to a low level at the polls in November. That same year, the American Legion Post issued a circular to town residents requesting contributions of clothing and food.

In November 1931, Morristown registered 150 persons out of work at the Mayor's Unemployment Relief Committee. "There was a big rush to file cards," one worker said. "All who filed were laborers and unskilled artisans, not white collar applicants, though many applied for assistance."

All those who sought work were not willing to take ordinary laboring jobs. In one month, four refused to do the jobs offered and one man worked a day and quit. To conserve funds, the Morristown Aldermen slashed salaries of town workers 7.25 to 15 percent, an action followed in 1932 by the board of education, which cut $30,722 in teachers' salaries. Proposed projects were put "on hold."

Many Morristown men and youth worked for the CCC mostly at the Jockey Hollow and Fort Nonsense areas of Morristown National Historic Park, removing dead timber, clearing slash and trees infected with the Dutch Elm disease, moving and planting 30,000 trees and shrubs, constructing gutters on roads in the Jockey Hollow area, and constructing replicas of the log huts the soldiers built during the winter of 1779 and 1780.

"Unemployment will be practically wiped out in Morristown," Mayor Potts said when 100 local men were put to work on improvement of Morristown National Historic Park under the newly created Civil Works Administration (CWA) program.

Federal dollars to fund the projects were funneled through agencies created by the Franklin D. Roosevelt administration to assist recovery from the Depression by providing jobs and undertaking public work projects. Agencies active in the Greater Morristown Area in addition to the CWA were the Emergency Relief Administration (ERA), Public Works Administration (PWA), Civilian Conservation Corps (CCC), and the Works Progress Administration (WPA).

At the same time, 60 Morristown and 10 Morris Township men went to work placing a rock bottom on Burnham Park Swimming Pool, one of two Federal aid projects approved for an immediate start. Forty of the men worked at the Brookside Reservoir site gathering rock and thirty at Burnham Park preparing the pool for the rock surface. They received 50¢ an hour for a 30-hour work week.

Additional men went to work the following week at Lidgerwood Field, the second project approved for an immediate start. Other projects followed, including the building of the dam at Speedwell Lake that had burst in a heavy rainstorm, draining the lake.

In 1933, as the burden of the Depression was easing in Morristown, Mrs. Robert D. Foote, wife of one of Morristown's leading millionaires, donated land on her estate in James Street for 73 community gardens. Combined they raised 47,720 pounds of produce ranging from cabbage, corn, and beets to tomatoes, and a wide variety of other vegetables. The following year, the federal ERA program provided seed for 12 common vegetables for the gardeners. Included were string beans, lettuce, corn, spinach, beets, and carrots.

Some of the federal funds employed hundreds of men to build the Morristown airport and construct a $200,000 museum and library at Morristown National Historic Park. It was the largest grant awarded parks in 22 states. Other funds went to clear the land, build replicas of soldiers' huts and a military hospital, improve roadways, and erect displays in the Jockey Hollow area of the park, restore Fort Nonsense, construct sewers in Morris Plains, and renovate and enlarge Greystone Park State Hospital.

Hundreds of cords of wood cut by CCC laborers at Jockey Hollow in 1934 were given to the Emergency Relief Committee for distribution among deserving Morristown families to heat their homes during the winter months.

Morristown, which spent $44,419 in relief assistance from October 1932 to 1933, saw the cost of relief work cut sharply as 1934 dawned. The drop from $5,000 to $3,425 a month was due in a large measure to the federally funded projects. Officials predicted even further cuts in succeeding months.

Area firms did what they could to help out during the Depression, not only keeping men employed, but also distributing foodstuffs. One firm, the O'Dowd Dairy Company, donated 21,000 free quarts of milk during 1932 alone.

## MORRISTOWN MUNICIPAL AIRPORT

The idea of a municipal airport for Morristown was first broached in 1931 when the town purchased the Normandy Water Company property, one year after the first county air meet at the Hanover Flying Field drew a crowd of 15,000 spectators.

The purchase included 200 acres of marshland in Hanover Township facing on Columbia Road between Morris Township and Florham Park. Officials termed most of the land fairly level, stating it would provide an ideal airport with the possibility of runways 1 mile long.

Need of a proper landing field in the greater Morristown area had been stressed for some time and officials indicated this was the chance to develop one with little expense since the town owned the land. They pointed out that the field held possibilities as a site for corporate aircraft, flying schools, and private planes.

A headline in the *Morristown Record* December 18, 1933 stated: "Start Morristown Airport Work; Total Cost To Be About $135,000." The start of work followed an inspection of the area by representatives of the United States Department of Commerce, which through the CWA funded the entire project. It was the first airport in the United States approved for such funding by the Department of Commerce.

Seen as a great step forward in the development of Morristown, the airport provided work for 200 men. Initial construction included two bituminous runways 150 feet wide and 4,000 feet long with a bituminous paved 50-foot-wide taxiway connecting the runways to a small apron area on the west side of the field. Four hangars, each housing ten aircraft, were constructed on the west side of the field in 1946.

*A Seeing Eye trainer is training a dog to guide the blind on the streets of Morristown. She will work with a string of ten dogs for four months. In the fifth month, she becomes a teacher to a blind student.*

A year earlier, a five-story control tower was constructed and high intensity lighting installed on one runway and medium intensity lighting on the other. Another hangar was built in 1961, plus a combination administration and maintenance building adjacent to the central parking apron.

In the following years, drainage facilities were improved, runways and taxiway pavement upgraded, one runway extended to 6,000 feet, and 200 acres of additional land purchased. Altogether a total of $860,000 was initially poured into the airport construction.

Commercial firms were quick to respond to the availability of the airport. In 1951, Continental Can Company built a hangar; in 1959, Cessna Aircraft Company erected a building; in 1960, Chatham Aviation, a hangar; in 1962, Blanchard Securities, Inc., a hangar; and in 1963, Eastern Aero Corporation, two hangars.

In 1950, when the North Korean Army started using Russian-made T-34 tanks, soldiers discovered the Bazooka shells they were using just bounced off the tanks. A call was issued for larger shells and Picatinny Arsenal, already testing such a shell, responded. As the larger shells were finished, they were trucked to Morristown Airport where waiting Army cargo aircraft were on standby to fly them across the Pacific.

By 1980, over 200 people were employed at the airport with a payroll exceeding $2 million.

## THE SEEING EYE

In 1930, Mrs. Harrison Eustis, president of the Seeing Eye dog guide school, announced that Morristown had been selected as a training ground for dogs to guide the blind. One year later, the Seeing Eye purchased the 49-acre Schnieder estate on Whippany Road, Whippany, including the mansion, barns, garage, and caretaker's cottage. Thirty-four years later, in 1965, the Seeing Eye moved to Washington Valley where it purchased "Tranquility," the estate of Walter Kemeys, as its world headquarters.

The Kemeys mansion was razed and a modern building erected to provide living accommodations for blind students while they were training with their dogs on Morristown's streets.

At first only German shepherds were used as guide dogs. Then trainers started experimenting with other breeds, including Dobermans, boxers, schnauzers, labradors, golden retrievers, and elkhounds.

The instructors' day began at 8 a.m. and ended at 6 p.m. He did not teach in the classroom, but on the streets of Morristown, both summer and winter, in all kinds of weather. He walked an average of 10 miles a day, 50 miles a week, 2,500 miles a year training the dogs with the blind.

After 10 days of training on the school grounds, the dogs and their blind students were taken into Morristown to walk on the sidewalks, cross the streets in front of traffic, and learn commands. They walked around ladders, over cracked

*This is a general view looking east of the 30-foot-deep depression bulldozed for Route 287 between Washington's headquarters and the George Washington School.*

and broken pavement, past angry and snarling dogs, through revolving doors, and rode in elevators. They entered banks, department stores, office buildings, and coffee shops.

The blind students came from every state in the Union, Puerto Rico, and Canada. They paid $150 for their first dog and $50 for each replacement.

## THE ROUTE 287 BATTLE

Pity poor little two-lane Route 202 if the super six-lane Interstate Route 287 had not been built to ease its curb-to-curb traffic, making its way at a snail's pace along the twisting rural byway from Benminster in Somerset County through Morristown to the the New York State line.

The ensuing battle to keep the throughway from slicing Morristown in half, a controversy that pitted community against community, drew immediate support from all segments of Morristown, which bitterly opposed the route through the town that would cut between General George Washington's headquarters, a national museum, and the George Washington School.

The 13-year battle went from court to court, to Governor Richard Hughes, the State Highway Department, state and federal legislators, the United States Bureau of Roads, the Freeholders, the board of education, and eventually the White House.

Originally three alignments were proposed, Alignment A, the one finally adopted, which sliced Morristown in half, and Alignments B and C, both of which traversed Morris Township east of Morristown.

Letters of sympathy poured into the town from total strangers. A *Kiplinger Magazine* headline put it this way: "Keep Your Town's Historic Landmarks, The Past Can Tell a Living Story if Bulldozers Don't Bury it First."

As early as 1962, headlines proclaimed: "Route 202 Cauldron Boiling Anew." That year, Alderman Victor Woodhull called upon the state legislature to introduce and support legislation making it impossible to construct with state funds any highway damaging a National Park property or any National Shrine and called for renewed vigor in the town's fight to prevent wholesale destruction of its residential and historic areas.

As he spoke, communities surrounding Morristown urged the State Highway Department to "proceed as speedily as possible" with construction of Route 287 through Morris County. Municipal mayors said citizens of the area were "anxious for a final determination of an alignment and an early start of construction."

In 1963, the State Highway Department selected Alignment A through Morristown, noting the roadbed would be sunk 30 feet below grade through Morristown to allow for several local road overpasses. Mayor J. Raymond Manahan fired back with claims that 87 homes would be demolished on the east side of Revere and other local roads and numerous streets would have to be abandoned. The tax-ratable loss was put in excess of $50,000.

Morristown residents had pinned their hopes to keep the highway out of Morristown on Governor Richard Hughes's campaign pledge promising to do everything he could to prevent it at a local Democratic $100-a-plate fundraising breakfast. He termed it "silly" to send highways through cities which would later have to be pieced together with Urban Renewal funds.

In 1963, the influential Washington Association of New Jersey threw its weight behind the fight against sending Route 287 past Washington's headquarters. Lawrence B. Howell of New Vernon, association president, stated, "287 has unfortunately become a political football. There is no question that it is necessary and will benefit some areas but be a detriment to others. We are not in favor of Plan A, B, or C; we are opposed to any plan which would be harmful to this site."

In his annual report to the National Park Service that year, Dr. Francis S. Ronalds, park superintendent, stated, "Our greatest problem is the threat to the headquarters posed by the new expressway."

By November 1963, hopes for a change in alignment A grew dimmer. In July, the State Highway Department announced that the U.S. Bureau of Roads had approved Alignment A, which had been under consideration since a 13-hour public hearing three years earlier at Fairleigh Dickinson University.

Large signs erected by the town started to appear by road sides. They stated: "The New Jersey State Highway Department Plans to Cut this Town in Half with a Super Highway which will not Benefit you or the Town. Save Morristown. Your Town May be Next."

Because many were beside county roads, the Board of Freeholders ordered their removal, terming them a traffic hazard.

In mid-1965, the Board of Education filed charges in the Appellate Division of Superior Court in Trenton seeking to prevent the alignment through Morristown because of damage it would do to the George Washington School, which would be 40 feet away from the highway. They also sought an appointment with President Johnson and other officials in Washington. Their action was followed by a suit by the town.

The beginning of the end was apparent. In July 1964, the National Park Service withdrew its objection to Route 287 following approval of the alignment by the Federal Bureau of Roads.

The fight carried on by the Board of Aldermen in the face of overwhelming odds came to a quiet end on September 13, 1965 at a regular meeting of the aldermen. Even in its official death, it remained somewhat controversial. The vote to withdraw a town-instituted court action to block the highway construction was 7 to 2.

"There is nothing more we can do to stop it other than what we have already done," Mayor Marco Stirone told the aldermen. "I'm still against the road, but if we have to have it, then we should make every effort to obtain the best possible concessions we can get from the state."

The last ditch effort was a half-hearted attempt by 34 residents to block the demolition by bulldozers of four homes on Howell Place, and the determined five-day stand of two sisters who refused to leave their home.

# 8. The Business District— Restoration and Revival

In the past two centuries, Morristown's business district has changed drastically, from a few stores selling bare necessities to high rise glass and steel office buildings, department stores, multi-story banks, financial brokerage firms, restaurants, law firms, and apartment complexes.

Penny candy is gone, along with the 25¢ quart of milk. But the mom and pop stores that sold these items at long-ago prices are still around, struggling to compete with the larger supermarkets and convenience stores. Some are winning the struggle. Unfortunately, most are not.

It's a new Morristown revived and restored to meet the needs of the twenty-first century.

Morristown's business district is a study in contrasts, not unlike a lot of other downtowns struggling to find a new place in a world of mega-malls, a shrinking retail market, and corporate downsizing. Stores close and vacancies persist, yet there are signs of a resurgence in Morristown. Long-time independent merchants toil to stay open while national chains like The Gap and Century 21, which go only where promising upscale demographics and strong market research lead them, opened their doors.

Speedwell Avenue, long ago the main drag in town, once again is upscale, one entire side lined with the towering office buildings and mini mall of Headquarters Plaza. Washington Street, on the opposite side of town, not too many years ago a row of many empty stores, is making a comeback with a huge apartment complex with stores on the first floor.

For years, the blot on the business district was the empty Macy's Department store, once Bamberger's, and half a block of empty stores on North Park Place, once the prime retail space around The Green.

In days gone by, there were horses and carriages, the delivery wagons that stopped at homes each morning for orders to be delivered before noon, and the trolley that once circled The Green.

Some early stores serviced customers by traveling to their homes on foot or horseback, often taking several days to make a trip, delivering merchandise and taking orders for the next trip. Later, horses and wagons sped up delivery, but it wasn't until 1915 that the roads were good enough for a steady flow of customers to come into town to make their selections.

Some provisions came to the doorsteps of houses in town. Cries of "Get your new June peas" and "Lettuce, fresh, crisp lettuce" heralded the arrival of the produce vendor's wagon. Its route started in the affluent neighborhoods, then moved on to Little Dublin and Little Italy, and the homes of servants and outdoor laborers.

Gas street lights and the old lamplighter who made his tour of the town at night and morning have been replaced by high-powered electric lights, replicas of the original gas lights.

Today it is different. There are traffic lights everywhere, electronically controlled to move the traffic in somewhat of a systematic pattern. But the backup of trucks and cars is there, moving at a snail's pace around The Green, many drivers hopelessly looking for an empty parking space.

Still, some of the buildings erected years ago remain facing The Green. Old-timers can pick their architecture out even if modern decor has changed the ground floor. But they too are fast disappearing.

Gone is the huge parking lot on Cattano Avenue that once was Macy's, replaced by a parking deck. Across the street from it the large town parking lot that once was jammed with parked automobiles is a large apartment complex, part of the renewal mix that is changing the face of the business district.

Indicative of the attraction of the new Morristown is the search by drivers for empty parking meters around The Green and the rapid filling up of parking lots. With the opening of the Century 21 Department Store in the vacant Macy Building, a whole new revival picture is envisioned by store owners, some of whom see nighttime shopping in Morristown as a possibility.

Compared to the business district at the turn of the century, the business district of today offers a far different picture. Then there were three hotels facing The Green, two on Washington Street, several on Speedwell Avenue, and one on South Street. Houses were mixed in between stores, and stables were located just off The Green.

The business district began on South Street at DeHart Street, and there was no Mid-Town Shopping Center on Morris Street, only scattered stores. A few shops were located on Market Street and other side streets. There were no parking lots, just hitching posts for horses and carriages.

But in those days there was curb service. A person in a carriage pressed a buzzer set into an iron post in front of a store, summoning a clerk to take an order.

Salny Brothers, one of the larger clothing stores, was founded in 1895 at the corner of High Street and Speedwell Avenue. It was a time when Speedwell Avenue was still a dirt road and one had to don boots to cross the thoroughfare after a heavy rain. In 1912, they moved to new and larger quarters across the street, and eventually to West Park Place facing The Green. Theirs is one of the stores affected by the Macy's closing. In their place now is The Gap.

Other early stores were Cranes Department Store on South Street, bought by Epstein; Jodo Gift Shop on North Park Place, which celebrated its 25th anniversary in 1969; Glick Hardware Store on Speedwell Avenue, a victim of the Urban Renewal project; Haimann's Jewelers on Washington Street, closed in 1977 after 57 years in business; Sears Robuck and Company, closed in 1978 when Rockaway Townsquare Mall opened; Roots Clothing Store on South Street at Headley Road, closed; and the Foster Market on South Street, a landmark, closed.

Three stores that celebrated 100 years in business in 1933 are gone. They included the Apothecary Shop founded by Frederick King in 1825; Voorhees Hardware Store founded in 1830 by Cook, Voorhees and Company; and George Green and Son, founded in 1837.

Two years earlier was the high water mark for chain groceries. At one time, they included the American Store, the Mutual Store, the A&P, the Great Eastern Store, and the National Store. Today, only the A&P and Kings Super Market remain.

A headline in the *Daily Record* told the story: "Chain Stores Reaching End of Development Cycle. Being Replaced by Super Markets." In 1930, Morristown had 34 chain stores. Today there are none.

One merchant on The Green is famous. He is W.F. Day, the confectioner, famous for catering, homemade ice cream and candies, and superb luncheons. His Town House on The Green is gone, the building in which it was located on West Park Place incorporated into the Epstein Department Store.

It was a place where patriots, politicians, and shoppers were treated to American cuisine since 1773. On the third floor, Henry Ward Beecher delivered speeches

*This street scene is at the intersection of North Park Place and Speedwell Avenue, and was painted c. 1860. This area is now the site of the Century 21 Department Store.*

*This picture shows South Street in 1908. The building in the background was the Babbitt Building, Morristown's skyscraper until Headquarters Plaza was built.*

against slavery and the names of Civil War draftees were picked from a hat. Huge ovens in the basement were where Milton Hershey learned the art of baking before he went on to manufacture his famous chocolate bars.

Diagonally across the street at the intersection of South Street with West Park Place was pharmacy corner, the location of a pharmacy since 1825 when Frederick King founded his apothecary shop, the same year Lafayette revisited Morristown.

The prescription department, which had been built up over the years, grew to be more than a drugstore. Through a succession of owners, it was looked upon as an institution, which drew medical and other customers from all parts of northern New Jersey

Old ledgers preserved for a century disclose the interesting remedies resorted to in 1853. Included were: Leeches, 25¢ each; Segars, 25¢ each; Dewees Mixture, 12¢ for 2 ounces; Godfrey's Cordial, 17¢ for 6 ounces; Turkish powder, rhubarb, $1.48 a quarter pound; Calomel and Opii, 24 pills, 22¢; Tinct Laudanum, 6¢ for one ounce; Brandy, 50¢ a quart, and Old Sherry wine, 62¢ a quart.

Every afternoon, the Otto H. Kahn children, Maud, Margaret, Gilbert, and Roger, could be seen with an English nanny in uniform and veil who drove them to Morristown in a fringed surrey. There at King's Drug Store, Eddie, who presided over the soda fountain, allowed each to mix his favorite ice cream soda or sundae.

The drugstore and its famous 35-foot-long soda fountain, for which an ice cream manufacturing plant had to be installed so large was the quantity of ice cream consumed, is gone now, replaced by a travel agency.

Across South Street was the F.W. Woolworth Store and its lunch counter, opened in 1912. The closing of the Woolworth eatery marked the end of an era in Morristown, an era during which the 4-booth, 18-seat lunch counter became a home away from home for many persons.

Earlier, there had been an attempt to modernize the old-fashioned setup. Spruced up menus were unveiled, a new specials board listed lunchtime features in brightly colored ink, and a stand-up sign outside the main entrance advertised grilled cheese sandwiches and Philly steak sandwiches. But it did not bring in many new customers.

One senior citizen who had been eating at Woolworths since she was a kid exclaimed: "Golly, you can't live without Woolworth's. I plan my day to come here around noontime. Oh yeah, there are other places, but they're so expensive. Social Security doesn't pay that much; I've got to watch my money, and Woolworth's fits into what I can afford."

Woolworth's, with its large Coffee Shop sign over the lunch counter, is gone, replaced by a Foot Locker sneaker store. Gone too is S.S. Kresge Company, the town's other five-and-dime store, once located on North Park Place.

Closing of the small stores, many because of increasing rents, others because the owners were retiring, brought many different reactions from customers. Typical was the Washington Market at 77 Washington Street. When it closed its doors in 1966 after more than 30 years, customers sat on stools and cried.

"You'd never believe it," said Ed G. Daher, who with his elder brother Joseph retired from the meat and fancy grocery business catering to customers all over Morris County. "We had three persons sitting there crying at the same time."

The start to put new life into Morristown's business district dates to the late 1980s. The town fathers had pinned their hopes for 15 years on a major urban renewal complex with offices, a hotel, and stores. It was finally built on Speedwell Avenue, but when the recession hit and downsizing followed, the office space fell vacant. That took away many shoppers. And eventually many of the retailers folded.

In 1994, in an effort to speed the turnaround, the Morristown Partnership was founded. Financed by an additional tax on businesses and property owners in the business district, it raised approximately $800,000 annually. The funds are used to bring in new businesses, keep the ones already there, and make the county seat more eye appealing.

With demographics that show a median income of $80,000 within a 3- to 10-mile radius, and 32 percent of the households within a 5- to 10-mile radius with incomes between $75,000 and $150,000, Morristown is poised for a resurgence.

Two men and their determination may be credited with helping to save Morristown. While the town's two other anchor stores, Macy's and Oppenheim Collins (later taken over by Franklin Simon, a block down South Street from

Epstein's) pulled up stakes, Epstein's confronted the problem head on. They opened satellite stores, primarily specializing in clothing for women and girls in the then-new Livingston Mall, and in Bridgewater and Princeton.

They hung on to the satellite stores until the early 1990s when financial problems forced them to retrench and close them. But they were not about to abandon the town in which Epstein's had been a name for a half-century. Especially since their almost block-long flagship store had been valued at $10 million in 1994.

By staying, they became the magnet for the next wave of stores. Slowly, the big chain stores like The Gap, Staples, Century 21, Starbucks, and The Gap Kids moved in.

Founded in 1911 by Maurice and Rose Epstein, Epstein's began as a small storefront apparel operation known as "The Fair" on Washington Street, selling blouses and baby clothing, most of which Rose hand-embroidered or knitted herself.

They moved to their present location in 1929 and, in 1968, started a $1-million expansion program, six years after opening their own parking lot. In came new marble floors, gleaming brass-rimmed glass display cases, mahogany woodwork, and a new way of organizing departments and displaying merchandise. They were named the "1975 Retailer of the Year" by the New Jersey Retail Merchants Association.

Epstein's was known for the Christmas window displays that received national recognition. They are best remembered for displays like Angel and her companions, the cherubs and their animal friends, Christmas in Morristown in 1779 when the town was General George Washington's headquarters, and the 1912 era, a display celebrating their 50th anniversary.

The theme of Colonial Morristown in 1779 included youngsters making and giving gifts to Continental soldiers, tree trimming on Sugar Loaf Hill, a kitchen scene in the Ford mansion, General Washington's headquarters, and a Christmas ball scene in Arnold Tavern.

Barney Field, the store's advertising manager, the man responsible for the displays, went to Williamsburg, Virginia to research the 1779 display. He was aided by Melvin Weig and Bruce Stewart of the Morristown National Historical Park.

One Christmas as the center window was opened, Field was standing beside the display featuring the little angel. He noticed an elderly woman reading the legend that went with that display. He knew that he had touched a chord of sympathy, for she wept as the sad impact of the display reached her.

In the early years, Epstein's made deliveries in a horse and wagon. On the side of the wagon was "M. Epstein, formerly The Fair, 31-38 Park Place, Morristown.

When Bamberger's opened in 1949, every customer on opening day got an orchid flown in from Hawaii. Newspaper accounts of the opening reported "one of the largest crowds ever to enter Morristown arrived in full force yesterday to attend the formal opening of the L. Bamberger & Co. store at Park Place and Speedwell Avenue."

*Bulldozers demolished buildings on the right-hand side of Speedwell Avenue, including the municipal building and a firehouse.*

In keeping with the Colonial tradition of Morristown, Bamberger's erected five huge medallions on the front of the building. Each represented one of the leading citizens of Morris County during the Colonial era with the artifacts for which they were most remembered.

Included was Jacob Ford, whose home Washington used as his headquarters, with the powder mill where powder was manufactured for the Continental Army; Lewis Morris, after whose family the county is named, with the old Morris County Courthouse on The Green; Betsy Schuyler, who was courted by young Alexander Hamilton, with the Schuyler-Hamilton House; John Doughty, one of the founders of the game of baseball, with cannon and shot; and Timothy Johnes, pastor of the Morristown Presbyterian Church, with the Bible and the old church. The medallions remain on the front of the building, now the Century 21 Department Store.

When the bulldozers moved in to wreck the buildings on the east side of Speedwell Avenue in 1971, it was the start of a new era in Morristown. The start came after four years of effort and twelve or more years of discussion on unsuccessful proposals. Bursting fireworks took the place of the traditional turning of the first shovel of earth for the initial 10-story office building aptly named "1776 on The Green."

Raymond DeChiara, Urban Renewal Director, termed "The father of the project" for his driving power without which it would not have materialized, noted "this is only the beginning." Senator Harrison A. Williams termed the groundbreaking "the beginning of a tomorrow that will preserve in this historic area the best of the past."

Few people realized that after the entire side of Speedwell Avenue was razed, there would appear a deep hole in the ground where the hotel and office buildings were to be erected. Surrounded by a high wooden fence on which were painted various figures, it was called by some "a town's nightmare."

But the worst was yet to come. The argument arose over who would finance construction of the 2,500-car parking garage, how many stages it would be built in, and who would build it. While the often-heated arguments continued between the town fathers, the management of the construction company, and DeChiara, town residents termed it "an albatross around the town's neck."

Financed in part by a federal grant, the 11-acre Urban Renewal Project included three towering office buildings, a three-level parking garage, a 40,000-square-foot split level theater, 260-room hotel, a health club, and shopping mall.

The project first considered in the 1960s, when parts of Speedwell Avenue were deteriorating, faced many hurdles ranging from who should be allowed to do what, how high the buildings should be, and how to go about removing the existing buildings. The difference spurred many lawsuits before an agreement was reached between the town and developers.

The recession hit hard at Headquarters Plaza. One of the first major tenants to go was AT&T, which occupied most floors in one of the office buildings. Others, including store owners in the mall, followed.

*This is an aerial view of the hole bulldozed for the foundations of Headquarters Plaza. Some residents termed the hole "a town's nightmare."*

# 9. Houses of Worship

Religion played an important role in life in Morristown in the 1800s and early 1900s, especially during the great revival period of 1827 and 1828. It was a time of serious devotion. In the beginning, before churches were erected in Morristown, people traveled as far as Elizabeth to worship. Services then did not last an hour or two as today, but could last all day Sunday, even into the evening hours when candles provided illumination in the sanctuary.

The first church in Morristown, the First Presbyterian Church, was erected facing The Green on property donated by Benjamin Hathaway and Jonathan Lindsley for a church, parsonage, and burial ground. Two other major churches, the Baptist Church erected on The Green and the Methodist Church on South Park Place facing The Green, followed.

Each ethnic group that settled in Morristown, whether the congregation was large or small, built churches, frame at first, then of stone and granite, most within a short distance of The Green.

Three of the major churches were destroyed by fire: the Second Presbyterian Church, the congregation of which was an offshoot of the First Presbyterian Church, the Methodist Church, and the Baptist Church. All were rebuilt.

Fire totally destroyed the frame Second Presbyterian Church on South Street January 8, 1877. The first firemen on the scene reported the flames had traversed the entire length of the building and were pouring out in livid masses from the bell tower.

A newspaper account of the blaze reported: "The entire male population of Morristown and many ladies stood on South Street and watched the church burn. The flames lit up the streets of the whole town," the article stated. "A newspaper could be distinctly read on the depot platform," several blocks away.

The firemen saved the parsonage; the library of the Sunday School, which was partly damaged; a piano and small organ; and some seats from the Sunday School. The main church organ was destroyed. Damage was estimated at $75,000.

The Norman-style Methodist Church was reduced to a hollow shell by a raging fire on January 22, 1972, the glow from which could be seen for miles. Firemen said the blaze appeared to have started in the basement stairwell between the boiler rooms and spread rapidly.

The 3-foot-thick Pudding Stone walls on two sides of the church and the twin towers, one 150 feet tall, remained standing. The sanctuary, Fellowship Hall, the choir loft, library, and valuable stained glass memorial windows which replaced the original windows in 1916 were reduced to rubble. Damage was estimated at more than $1 million.

The sterling silver Communion Set, memorial plaques, silver tea and coffee services, many pieces of silver flatware, and an altar table were reclaimed from the ashes and mass of wet, blackened timber.

Prior to reconstruction, the 600-family congregation voted down a movement to move the church from The Green to a site at Lake and Sussex Avenues. Demolition of all but the front wall and towers started 18 months after the fire. The one-year rebuilding at a cost of $1,523,619 resulted in a compromise of the traditional and the contemporary with long curving arches supporting a high vaulted roof of ponderosa pine.

On May 21, 2000, the 108-year-old Baptist Church on Washington Street, opposite the Morris County Courthouse, was ravaged by flames, five hours before parishioners were to gather for Sunday services.

The first firemen on the scene reported they could see "a large volume of fire shooting skyward through the roof" of the Gothic-style building that had been covered with ivy. "The fire had a big head start," firemen reported. A 110-foot-tall Belleville tower between the sanctuary and the church offices was left standing after the fire. But most of its stained glass windows were blown out. Firefighters from Morristown, Morris Township, Florham Park, Morris Plains, and Cedar Knolls poured tons of water on the fire. As they hosed smoldering sections of the thick slate roof, portions of it collapsed, dislodging beams and overhanging eaves.

By mid-2002, the church was being rebuilt. The fire did more than displace parishioners, some of whom lived as distant as Morris Plains and Newton. The church served also as headquarters for several social service agencies and a Hispanic Baptist congregation that used church rooms for services.

## FIRST PRESBYTERIAN CHURCH

Morristown's first church, a small wooden building, nearly square with shingled sides, was erected by the First Presbyterian Church, an offshoot of the Presbyterian Church of Hanover, *c.* 1740. When the frame had been raised, a small platform of boards with a chair and small table served for a pulpit. Congregation members were seated on windowsills and other timbers.

In 1764, the church trustees granted permission to erect a steeple 125 feet in height. In it was hung a bell, the gift, tradition says, of the King of Great Britain. It had on it the impress of the British Crown and the name of the makers, Lister & Pack of London. The bell was recast in 1860 and again in 1895. Hence the local rhyme:

"Little Church, Tall Steeple;
"Little Town, Proud People."

144

The increasing number of members made enlargement of the building a necessity in 1774. A still further increase in membership and the hard use to which the building was put as a smallpox hospital during the Revolutionary War, soon made a new, larger church mandatory. Plans were drawn for a frame church 75 feet long and 55 feet wide with a steeple 20 feet square at its base.

The old church was purchased by Morris County Sheriff Oscar Lindsley, whose great-grandfather donated the land on which the church was built. Hundreds of people gathered to see the steeple taken down, many of whom took shingles as souvenirs. Lindsley took the church in pieces to Green Village and erected it as a barn near Woodland Road.

The steeple was preserved and stands today in a corner of the burial ground where at least 158 Revolutionary War soldiers are buried, the majority in mass graves. The weathervane of the steeple was taken down and given to the old academy in New Vernon.

In 1893, the present stone church was erected on East Park Place, nine years after the stone parsonage was erected at a cost of $14,670.

## FIRST BAPTIST CHURCH

The second church erected in Morristown was the First Baptist Church, the 11-member congregation of which first met in 1752 in a frame building on Mt. Kemble Avenue, about 3 miles from Morristown, opposite the entrance to Sand Spring Road. In 1771, when the congregation had increased to 85 members, a new church was erected on the northwest corner of The Green. It did not have a spire or chimney.

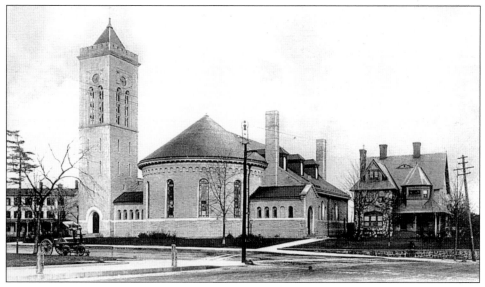

*The First Presbyterian Church, the first church erected in Morristown, is on East Park Place. The parsonage was built in 1884 and the chapel in 1869.*

*The First Baptist Church, built on The Green in 1771, moved to Washington Street in 1897. The church, gutted by fire in 2000, was rebuilt.*

Like the First Presbyterian Church, it served as a smallpox hospital for Revolutionary soldiers in 1777. After 70 years, the congregation decided to build a new house of worship at Littleton. In 1840, they offered the meeting house and lot to the Second Presbyterian Church for $2,500, reserving the cemetery. The committee, however, demanded a part of the cemetery, a condition the Baptists would not agree to, so the negotiations fell through.

The Baptists commenced the erection of a new meeting house on Park Place and Speedwell Avenue, now the site of the Century 21 Department Store. Portions of the McAlpin Block stood on the site of the adjacent graveyard dating to the Revolutionary War. The cemetery continued in use until the turn of the century when McAlpin bought the property and removed the bodies to Evergreen Cemetery.

Many topics were discussed by the ministers of the different churches, some good, some bad. Typical were the sermons preached against horse races on South Street and Madison Avenue, talks which indirectly led to the founding of the South Street racetrack. It too came under fire for gambling on horse races.

Perhaps the strongest sermon was one delivered in the Baptist Church against the sale of liquor to children and gambling.

In 1897, Reverend Samuel Zane Batten stood in the pulpit with five bottles of whiskey beside the Bible in front of him. He had announced that he would preach on "the liquor traffic in Morristown," sending invitations to every saloon keeper and hotel owner to attend the service.

"This bottle," he said, holding up one labeled "Rye Whiskey," "was purchased at a hotel by a 14-year-old boy on last Sunday afternoon. Here's another purchased since 7 o'clock last night at a leading drug store without a prescription. The other three bottles were bought at different hotels last Sunday."

"The law is being violated daily and nightly. The Citizen's League has evidence at first hand of scores of violations. This will be at the disposal of the grand jury next week. If no indictments follow, we'll known who is to blame."

Turning to another subject, he said, "this town is fairly alive with gambling. Within a stone's throw of this church a poker game is now in progress. One third of the boys in Morristown over 14 gamble. We can't fix the responsibility. Both the mayor and police disclaim responsibility under the present charter. Then let us change the charter tomorrow."

Several saloon keepers listened in silence. Present also were Sheriff E.L. Durling, Assistant U.S. District Attorney Thomas J. O'Brien, Prosecutor J.S. Salmon, and Mayor Edward A. Quale.

The following year, 1888, the congregation decided to sell the property on Park Place and move to Washington Street, where the cornerstone of the burned out church was laid in 1897 on property costing $67,000.

## THE UNITED METHODIST CHURCH

The third church in Morristown was erected by the Methodists in 1827 opposite the Farmer's Hotel in Market Street at the corner of Maple Avenue. A two-story brick structure, 40 feet by 60 feet in size with a gallery on three sides, it served until 1841 when a white frame church was built. The initial service was held in the Morris Academy and subsequent services, pending completion of the first church building, in the session room of the First Presbyterian Church.

Growing rapidly in numbers and influence, the Methodist Church added more than 200 names to its congregation during the great revival of 1827 and 1828. This was a period of great religious feeling and stores were closed for several days, the people devoting themselves to religious matters.

In 1866, George T. Cobb, a millionaire iron capitalist, gave the site on South Park Place for a new church to which he contributed $100,000. He purchased the old frame building and, as a gift from his family, turned it over to the African Methodist Church. It was towed in Morris and Spring Streets by oxen to its new site in Spring Street.

At the time, the new edifice was considered one of the most magnificent structures in this part of the country. Built of purple pudding stone gathered from a Parsippany farm and carefully cut to bring out the purple color, it had a seating capacity of 1,100 persons. The trimmings were of Maine granite. Towering over the entrance is a 150-foot-tall spire and smaller tower. In January 1975, the carillon chimes in the tower were heard again. The 100-bell Mass-Rowe carillon installed after the fire, sounds Westminster chimes at regular intervals as well as hymns several times daily.

Earlier, in 1962, before the fire, the church began construction of a third-floor addition to house its offices and church social rooms. This time, however, the pudding stone was collected from the property of church members.

The space in front of the church, in which the Newark Conference was organized and celebrated its golden jubilee in 1907, was once enclosed by a high wrought iron fence with tall urns containing flowers.

## SAINT PETER'S EPISCOPAL CHURCH

In the Gilded Age, they called Saint Peter's Episcopal Church, "The Church of the 100 millionaires." The irreverent went so far as to term it "the Morris County Golf Club on its knees," inferring that its congregation was comprised basically of the socially elite members of the county club.

It was.

Everyone who was anyone belonged to it. Here were held some of society's most elaborate weddings, including that of Sylvia Green, daughter of Hettie Green, the world's richest woman, whom the press had tabbed "The Witch of Wall Street." In her will, Mrs. Green bequeathed the church $1.2 million.

Prior to 1828, services were held at Macculloch Hall and in the Baptist Church. The cornerstone of the first Saint Peter's Episcopal Church was laid November 14, 1828, one year after the parish was established. By the mid-1800s, accommodations in the red brick edifice were becoming increasingly inadequate despite an altering and enlargement of the church in 1858. This need for more room to seat the congregation led to a movement in 1883 to start a fund drive for a new church.

By 1886, $40,000 had been raised and on Easter Sunday, 1887, ground was broken for the new edifice designed by the New York architectural firm of McKim, Mead & White. Two years later, the old building was taken down and the foundation laid for the tower of the new Saint Peter's.

The wealthy not only donated to the building fund, they also gave generous material gifts ranging from stained glass windows to colorful banners and a classical font. In its graveyard are buried many of the prominent people of the "Gilded Age." Included are names such as Stephen and Alfred Vail, the Ogdens, Canfields, Colles, Keasbeys, and Samuel V. Hoffman, the donor of the church parish house erected on South Street in 1897.

Among donors to the building fund were John T. Foote, who later purchased a burial plot for $1,000; Eugene S. Higgins, George G. Kip, and Richard A. McCurdy.

Initially, land for the church between Maple and Macculloch Avenues was first donated by John Boykin, for whom Boykin Street was named (now Miller Road). John D. Canfield offered to donate the stone, which was quarried and piled on the Boykin Street lot. Just as ground was about to be broken for the church, a more

*The United Methodist Church was built on East Park Place in 1866 on land donated by George T. Cobb, a millionaire who contributed $100,000 to the building fund. Gutted by fire in 1972, it was rebuilt.*

suitable site was offered for sale on South and Boykin Streets. The lot given by Boykin was reconveyed to him.

Actual construction of the church took a period of years during which the nave was enlarged and new tower plans drafted to make it taller to achieve architectural balance. It was finally finished in 1907.

All pews were put up for auction and sold to the highest bidder, a practice in vogue at the time. Prices ranged from $100 to $150. Pew holders paid an annual charge of 12 percent on the purchase price, the assessment being increased from time to time to meet budgetary needs.

The rectory was built in 1914, replacing an old rectory razed in 1900. The new rectory faced South Street next to the church. At that time, a central heating system was installed in the church.

During construction, a long wooden shed was erected at one end of the property. In it, 18 stonecutters worked cutting the stone blocks to size. At the other end, two blacksmiths continually sharpened and repaired their tools.

In 1907, Mrs. L. Heyworth Mills offered to have carved a statue of Saint Peter to place in the niche in the front of the tower, 66 feet above the ground. It was sculptured in Italy. In 1947, workmen discovered the head of the statue had broken loose from the body. It could not be repaired and was removed and taken to a communicant's farm where it was buried.

In 1960, Mrs. William T. Kirk offered to replace the 8-foot-tall statue of Saint Peter. It was carved from an 8-ton block of close-grained granite quarried in Vermont, a job that took four months to complete. It weighs 3 tons.

The bell of the old church was too small for use in the new tower. In 1922, Mrs. William B. McVicker visited the John Taylor Foundry in Loughborough, England, and purchased a large bell. Considered part of a future carillon of 37 bells made in England and donated by congregation members, they sat on the parish lawn, guarded at night by a watchman until hung in the tower. They were dedicated in 1924. They weighed 21,008 pounds.

## CHURCH OF THE REDEEMER

The idea of forming a second Episcopal congregation in Morristown was started in 1852 by a small group of communicants who broke off from Saint Peter's Episcopal Church to form the Church of The Redeemer. The initial meetings were held in the Morris Academy with a lay reader serving in the absence of an ordained minister.

Plans and a lot at Market and Pine Streets, opposite the railroad station, on which to build the Church of The Redeemer were secured during the winter and construction started on a frame building in the form of a cross in the spring.

*The Church of The Redeemer was built in 1886 by a small group who left Saint Peter's Church. The present edifice was erected in 1917.*

In 1886, a lot was purchased on South Street and the church building moved up Pine Street and across fields to the South Street site. A residence that occupied the front of the lot was moved to the rear and altered to serve as a rectory, pastor's study, and Sunday School.

Originally, the church lot belonged to the First Presbyterian Church, which owned all the land on the East side of South Street from The Green to Pine Street. The lot purchased by the Church of The Redeemer was designated as "the parsonage lot."

The present Gothic stone edifice constructed of light-tinted granite and the parish house were erected in 1917.

The bell hung in the tower of the frame church was the gift of Mrs. Stella H. Peck in memory of her husband Lorraine T. Peck, a vestryman and founder of the Peck School. Prayer books for the chancel were donated by Mrs. August Belmont, a communion service by Mrs. Peter Stuyvesant, and the organ and other furnishings by several ladies of the congregation.

In 1958, a 44-inch-diameter bell cast in Annecy, France was placed in the belfry in the north corner of the church.

## SECOND PRESBYTERIAN CHURCH

The Second Presbyterian Church was a child of the First Presbyterian Church and the fifth church to be built in Morristown. It was formed January 26, 1841 when a paper signed by 141 persons was presented at a meeting of the Session of the First Presbyterian Church.

It stated: "We, the subscribers, respectfully request of the Session of the First Presbyterian Church, Morristown, a dismission from said church, with a recommendation to the Second Presbyterian Church to be organized in Morristown." At a subsequent meeting of the session on June 8, 1841, 60 other persons requested dismission. Both requests were granted.

Of the total initial congregation of the Second Presbyterian Church, 207 of the 208 members were from the First Presbyterian Church.

The first service was held in the Morris Academy prior to a decision in 1841 to erect a house of worship. After purchasing the South Street site at a cost of $2,500, the congregation sent their teams, wagons, carts, and men to aid in the construction work. The cellar was dug and the sand taken from it used to fill a bog-hole on the 1.6-acre tract. Stone was quarried and hauled to the site, and timber, most of which was from the big swamp, was sawed at a sawmill near Green Village.

A bell to hang in the square tower was presented to the church by Judge Stephen Vail, and a clock and Bible by his wife.

## CHURCH OF THE ASSUMPTION

The Church of The Assumption, the first Catholic Church to be built in Morristown, was a small wooden building on Maple Avenue at the corner of Madison Street seating 300 persons.

At that time, the nearest Catholic Church was in Madison, which many people living at a distance as great as 20 miles attended, often traveling on foot.

The first meeting of the church congregation in 1847 was held in the Morris Academy. The church was located on the edge of the Little Dublin section of Morristown where many Irish families who worked on the estates had settled. The congregation, at first too poor to support a pastor, depended upon the services of a pastor from Madison. A pastor was finally stationed in Morristown, but he also had charge of congregations in Mendham and Basking Ridge.

When the Morristown congregation grew too large for one pastor to handle three parishes, a pastor was assigned permanently to the Church of The Assumption. As membership grew, the small wooden building became inadequate and it was used as a Sunday School. A new church of red brick, 122 feet long by 52 feet wide, was built. A steeple, 125 feet high capped by a spire over a peaked slate roof laid in ornamental colored bands, rose to a sharp point surmounted by a stone cross. The pews of the church seat nearly 1,000 persons. Cost of the building was $40,000.

*The Second Presbyterian Church was built on South Street by a group who left the First Presbyterian Church in 1841. It burned in 1877. The two churches eventually reunited.*

# 10. The Suburban Sprawl

When the boys came marching home from World War II, the greater Morristown area experienced a vast explosion in population, swept along by the GI Bill that guaranteed low cost mortgages for veterans. A countryside once dotted with pastures, orchards, and estates suddenly blossomed with subdivisions of new, low cost homes, apartment complexes, and in the 1980s, condominiums.

By 1965, garden apartments were built on both sides of the tracks and on lower South and Elm Streets. Real estate men gambled and won on construction of Lidgerwood and Robert Morris Park developments, and the Federal government erected low and middle-income housing in the Pocahontas Lake area.

In Morris Township during the 1960s, 16 former millionaires' estates were subdivided into housing developments in Convent Station, Normandy Heights, and on Sussex and Park Avenues. They were followed by apartment complexes on Madison Avenue, Whippany Road, and Speedwell Avenue.

With the population boom came scientific industry; office buildings, many on former estates on Madison Avenue; corporate headquarters; light manufacturing facilities; communications and publishing industries; insurance and real estate companies; and legal and consulting firms. Many were Fortune 500 companies.

By 1975, the greater Morristown area was no longer a bedroom community for New York. Business and industry discovered the area in the late 1950s as overcrowded city facilities demanded more air, light, and room to grow. Attracted by a ready supply of potential employees, select firms started moving into the area, building vast corporate headquarters, some in industrial parks. Others followed.

In the 1940s, Allied Signal Corporation established a research laboratory on the former Otto Kahn estate, which grew into their world headquarters. In 1952, General Drafting Company, makers of road maps and publishers, bought "Glynallan," George Marshall Allen's estate, for its national headquarters. In 1953, the Mennen Company, makers of beauty and health care products, moved its plants and headquarters from Newark, settling on the former Eugene Higgins estate. In 1969, textbook publishers Silver Burdett located beside Route 287.

These are only a few of the industries and corporate headquarters that selected the greater Morristown area. Others include such firms as Warner Lambert Pharmaceutical Company (Now Pfizer Company), Bell Telephone Laboratories,

Sandoz Pharmaceutical Company, Westinghouse, Flintkote Company, Automatic Switch Company, Nabisco, and Travelers Insurance Company. Many of the names of the original firms have changed over the years due to takeovers, buy outs, and consolidation.

To serve the increased population, the Morristown business center expanded, new stores opened, municipal services were increased, and educational, cultural, banking, and recreational facilities were expanded.

The Morristown of 250 residents that General George Washington brought his Continental Army to in 1777 is changing, almost daily, in appearance. Huge apartment complexes have sprung up in the business center, townhouses with private elevators, two fireplaces, and two-car garages are being built in the Morristown Historic District, and new parking garages cater to hundreds of shoppers.

Today, everywhere one looks, especially in Morris Township, new homes are going up, more than 75 percent of them in subdivisions. In space-starved Morristown, it is a different story. There are few lots left, but most of the construction is of apartments and townhouses.

The development of increased housing in Morristown dates to the 1920s when the large estates started to break up. One development, Sherman Park, which started out to be a copy of Tuxedo Park in Orange County, New York, developed by Pierre Lorillard of tobacco fame in 1886, was once "Ridgewood Hall," the estate of Dr. Frederick H. Humphreys, nicknamed the "Patent Medicine King."

In 1929, it was subdivided into 122 plots and 4 houses were built on lots sold at one of the earliest public auctions of estate property in the greater Morristown area. Others included "Audley Farms" in Mendham in 1946. Trains brought potential buyers from the city to the huge tents erected for the Sherman Park auction, which included land on Sussex Avenue, Speedwell Place, Cutler, Mills, and intersecting streets.

The original covenants, still in effect today, read like something out of eighteenth-century New England, such as no fences allowed to surround one's property, and no housing of chickens, ducks, or other livestock. Also not allowed: stores, foundries, or manufacturing of any kind.

The fate of the razed mansions is echoed throughout the town limits where scores of estates were demolished to provide expansion room for commercial, cultural, and residential facilities. Included are the once-great estates of Frederick Burnham, attorney for the Mutual Life Insurance Company; Patrick Farrelly; Admiral Cooper; Dr. Frederick H. Humphries; Samuel S. Freeman; Henry M. Olmstead; Georgiana C. Stone; Henry W. Ford; Charles E. Noble; and Mrs. William H. Howland. In their place have developed vast apartment complexes, real estate subdivisions, shopping centers, Morristown High School, the Jewish Center, and Morristown Memorial Hospital.

Typical was the Burnham homestead razed in 1962 for the 74-unit Lakeview Apartment complex. The story behind the disappearance of many of the other great homes is similar. "Woodley" on Madison Avenue, the half frame, half stone Edward A. Day mansion built in 1897, was razed in 1936 for a six-home subdivision, and "Fair Oakes," the estate of Mrs. Stone on Washington Avenue in 1920, for a subdivision of homes in the $15,000 to $17,000 class, some of them partially constructed with lumber from the wrecked Stone mansion. Others included the Ballantine, Pitney, Forbes, and Vernam mansions on Madison Avenue, all of which gave way to apartment or office complexes.

Until after World War II, there was no large-scale developments of houses. In Morristown, where building lots were scattered throughout the town, a single small house would be constructed, sometimes with, sometimes without a garage.

The greatest population growth took place between 1960 and 1970. By 1990, there were about three times as many people in the township where land was plentiful compared to 1940, the result of large-scale subdivision and apartment complex building.

As early as 1959, Morristown realized, "it is becoming more apparent each day that the center of Morristown is becoming impossibly congested; that traffic, trying to force its way through town, is increasingly inflating residential areas; and that, if positive action is not taken to provide the central commercial area with a proper solution, and the type of shopping ease and pleasure afforded by the new integrated, regional shopping centers, Morristown is going to be drastically hurt economically."

By 1966, as the population soared, 80 percent of the land in Morristown was developed compared to 60 percent in Morris Township and 50 percent in Morris Plains. Reasons for the population growth vary, but four stand out: attractiveness as a place to live, work, and play; strategic location in relation to major transportation arteries; vacant land and relative lack of open space in older city centers; and an overall trend toward decentralization of residences, industry, and business.

*Ridgewood Hall, the Victorian-style mansion of Dr. Frederick H. Humphries, known as the "patent medicine king," is in Sherman Park. He bought the 7.2-acre estate in 1890 from Mrs. Byron Sherman for $45,000.*

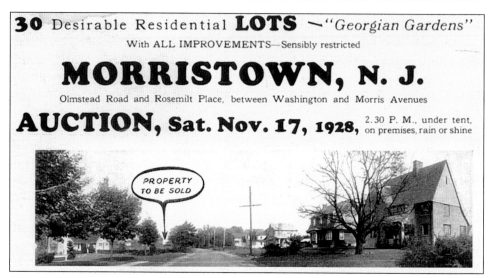

*This auction flyer is for the sale of lots in Georgian Gardens, between Washington and Morris Streets.*

Three major highways bisect Morristown. Route 24, the old Morris Turnpike, circles The Green and heads west on Washington Street to Mendham, Chester, and Warren County; Route 202 traverses Speedwell Avenue and North Park Place and heads south on Mt. Kemble Avenue; and Route 287 cuts the town in half with three exit and entrance ramps.

By 1979, single family homes, only a smattering in developments, accounted for 34 percent of the town's housing units; two, three, and four family units, 31 percent; garden apartments and townhouses, 23 percent; and larger apartment buildings, 12 percent. Then Morristown housing was considered old. A total of 54 percent was built before 1940. During the 1940s, 11.7 percent was built, a figure which rose in the period from 1950 to 1970, when a small building boom produced 14.8 percent. In 1979, Morristown and Morris Township experienced an influx of middle and upper-class residents from the central cities, many of whom at first were commuters to New York, but then switched to work in area world headquarters, laboratories, and research-oriented industries that were being attracted to the area. Among the first were the Allied Signal Corporation, General Drafting, and The Mennen Company.

Census figures show that Morristown's population of 16,189 in 1990 is declining. The figure for 2000 was 18,544 due largely to an influx of apartment residents. In contrast, Morris Township, with a population of only 2,284 in 1920, has soared upward as large apartment, single family homes, condominium, and townhouse complexes were built, mostly in the Convent, Normandy Heights, and Butterworth farms areas.

In 1973, Township Mayor James R. Leva said the planning and zoning boards had done well in the past in striking a balance between commercial and residential land use as the township serged ahead of Morristown in population numbers. He said the township now has its "needed ratables" and must concern itself with the larger problem of protecting its residents.

As early as 1966, it was "strongly recommended that Madison Avenue be developed as single family housing," a recommendation that did not fully come to pass. Today, it is lined in both Morristown and Morris Township with scattered single family houses, a housing complex, office buildings, a hospital, a restaurant, a quick food outlet, gasoline station, a convent, apartment complexes, and a church.

Today, the township has about three times the number of residents and four times the number of roads it had in the 1940s. It is about 60 percent residential, 32 percent commercial, and 8 percent parks and open space. Each section of the township has a personality of its own.

Washington Valley, perhaps the least built-up section, is a combination of marshes, wetlands, meadows, and woods protected by a vast watershed. The newer office buildings are in the eastern and southern sections of the township, many along Madison Avenue.

County parks abound throughout the eastern, northern, and southern sections of the greater Morristown area. In the northern section is the William G. Mennen Sports Arena built by the Morris County Park Commission on land donated by the Mennen Company, and the Frelinghuysen Arboretum with its Joseph F. Haggerty Jr. Education Center. The arboretum is the headquarters of the Park Commission.

At the entrance to Washington Valley is Fosterfields, New Jersey's first living historical farm operated by the Park Commission, and on the Mendham Road, one of the commission's most popular parks and swimming areas, Lewis Morris Park and Sunrise Lake. At the end of South Street on the site of the old racetrack is Seaton Hackney Park, donated to the Park Commission by Mrs. Paul Moore for a county riding academy.

Dedicated people, technological innovation, and commitment to quality backed by an influx of high-quality department stores, banks, financial institutions, and legal offices, insure Morristown's future as the hub of northern New Jersey's marketplace. It started with five high-rise steel and glass office buildings and spread in the dawn of the present century to apartment and townhouse complexes, an ever-increasing number of banking institutions, as well as improved health care facilities and arts, education, and social agencies.

Still more is to come, especially apartment house complexes, some in the business center, others on the town's fringes. They combine with modern interstate highways, public transportation, a skilled labor pool, and economic and demographic forecasts to provide a new Morristown without harming its Colonial tradition.

The present 60,000 to 80,000 people entering Morristown daily to work and shop, and the more than 100,000 visitors who annually visit the Morristown National Historical Park and the town's half-dozen museums, is expected to multiply in the next decade.

# Bibliography

Colles, Julia Keese. *Authors and Writers Associated with Morristown*. Morristown: Vogt Brothers, 1895.

Cox, Elbert. *Winter Encampments of the American Revolution*. National Park Service, 1941.

Hartwell, Dickson. *The Story of The Seeing Eye*. New York: Dodd, Mead & Company, 1942.

Hoskins, Barbara. *Washington Valley: An Informal History*. Ann Arbor, MI: Edwards Brothers, Inc., 1960.

Langstaff, John B. *New Jersey Generations*. New York: Vantage Press, 1964.

Lewis Historical Publishing Co. *A History of Morris County*. New York, 1914.

Munsell, W.W. *History of Morris County, New Jersey*. New York: W.W. Munsell & Company, 1882.

Putnam, Peter. *The Triumph of The Seeing Eye*. New York: Harper & Row, 1963.

Rae, John W. and John W. Jr. *Morristown's Forgotten Past: The Gilded Age*. Morristown: self published, 1979.

Rae, John W. *Thomas Nast, The Man Who Drew Santa Claus*. Morristown: self published, 1980.

————. *People Who Made Morris County*. Morristown: Morris County Board of Chosen Freeholders, 1986.

Sparkes, Boyden, and Moore, Samuel Taylor. *The Witch of Wall Street*. New York: Doubleday, Doran & Company, Inc., 1930.

Thayer, Theodore. *Colonial and Revolutionary Morris County*. Morristown: Compton Press, 1975.

Tomlinson, Norman B. *Fires of The Past in Morristown*. Morristown: The Daily Record Print, 1926.

Weig, Melvin J. *Morristown National Historical Park*. National Park Service, 1950.

## Newspapers

*The Democratic Banner*

*Evening Express*

*The Jerseyman*

*Genius of Liberty*

*Star Ledger* (Newark)

*Newark News*

*Daily Record*

*Morristown Topics*

# INDEX